Confessions of a Difficult Woman

Confessions of a Difficult Woman

the RENÉE GEYER story

By Renée Geyer
and Ed Nimmervoll

HarperCollins*Publishers*

HarperCollins_Publishers_

First published in Australia in 2000
by HarperCollins_Publishers_ Pty Limited
ACN 009 913 517
A member of the HarperCollins_Publishers_ (Australia) Pty Limited Group
http://www.harpercollins.com.au

HarperCollins_Publishers_
25 Ryde Road, Pymble, Sydney NSW 2073, Australia
31 View Road, Glenfield, Auckland 10, New Zealand
77–85 Fulham Palace Road, London W6 8JB, United Kingdom
Hazelton Lanes, 55 Avenue Road, Suite 2900, Toronto, Ontario M5R 3L2
and 1995 Markham Road, Scarborough, Ontario M1B 5M8 Canada
10 East 53rd Street, New York NY 10022, USA

National Library of Australia Cataloguing-in-Publication data:

Geyer, Renée, 1954- .
Confessions of a difficult woman: the Renée Geyer story.
ISBN 0 7322 6563 0.
1. Geyer, Renée, 1954- . 2. Women singers – Australia – Biography. 3. Singers – Australia –
Biography 4. Popular music – Australia. 5. Jewish families – Australia.
I. Nimmervoll, Ed (Edward Francis).
II Title.
781.63082092

Every effort has been made to trace the original source of copyright material
contained in this book. On behalf of the author, the publishers would be grateful
to hear from any copyright owners they have been unable to contact and
apologise for any errors or omissions.

Cover photo: Mushroom / Norman Seefe
Various photos are reproduced with kind permission of Mushroom Records

Printed in Australia by Griffin Press Pty Ltd on 79gsm Bulky Paperback

7 6 5 4 3 2 1   00 01 02 03 04

To My Parents

ACKNOWLEDGMENTS

When Alison Urquhart from HarperCollins first approached me about doing an autobiography, my first reaction was, *Why?* and, *Who'd care?* However, being the deeply shallow woman that I am, after much flattery (thank you Alison) and the promise of good things to come, I eventually caved in.

When the deal was finalised, the magnitude of the project dawned on me: *Where do I begin?* I asked Ed Nimmervoll, a trustworthy friend and respected music writer, to help me. Thankfully he said yes, and after many interviews and chats, Ed put together a rough draft of my life and career for me to have a look at. It was the first time I realised that maybe there was a little story to be told here, after all. I took it from there, basically telling the story from my perspective and adding little stories as they came to mind.

Thank you, Ed, for being a loyal friend and creating the framework for this book and then allowing me to play with it.

The editing process was a real learning experience, and I thank Susan Gray for persevering with me throughout the entire project with patience and understanding.

Thanks also to Odette Snellen for additional editorial assistance.

Finally, I'd like to thank friends and family who have helped me with information and pictures when I needed them, and a few of my brave buddies who had strong opinions about this book and didn't baulk when I asked for their two cents' worth.

Thanks to you all.

Renee xxx

Renee Geyer
c/o Walkaway Productions
PO Box 2271
Prahan Victoria 3181

www.reneegeyer.com.au

CONTENTS

FOREWORD

For those average punters who listen to the radio and wander into record shops to put their money where their hearts lie, music is about joy and memories.

The joy of first hearing a voice, a tune, a lyric which reaches deep inside and touches the heart and soul. The memories, so complex and rich, which are retrieved, often years later, when once again a piece of music is heard. A night in a club, a night of passion, a day on the beach, a moment when love was in the air, a happily drunken party – these are the moments to be treasured, and the music that goes with them becomes the soundtrack to everyone's private, and deeply personal, movie.

It is a measure of Renée Geyer's stature that every Australian (at least everyone who really cares about great music) has a number of Renée Geyer songs in their personal soundtrack. This remarkable woman with her rich, passionate, soulful, husky, exuberant, sensitive, dynamic voice has been with us now for ... oh my God, don't say it ... over a quarter of a century!

If you were around in 1974 you will treasure 'It's a Man's Man's World' – not James Brown's assertion of African American masculinity, but Renée's much more clever, feminine and ambiguous version. It was her first hit and those opening bars, together with that wonderful, in-your-face voice, have travelled down the years so well.

Then there are all those marvellous party songs – 'Heading in the Right Direction' (can you really recall the summer of 1975 without it?), the hauntingly beautiful 'Stares and Whispers' and the equally irresistible 'Say I Love You' – and beyond them there is the constant reminder that Renée is one of this country's greatest voices. She could sing the electoral roll and make it sound sexy. She has a real richness and passion which is rare in Australian singing. Of course her reference points are the great American gospel and soul singers, but she has not retreated to easy imitation. She has understood what makes soul and blues singing so special – the fact that every note, every breath, every space is imbued with real emotion – and she has given those qualities to her own performance.

So, after thirty years, what are we left with? Renée is probably the greatest popular singer Australia has ever produced. (OK! then name one who is better – and who is still around after more than a quarter of a century!) It all comes down to great songs sung in such a way that they connect with those who listen and care to respond. We are emotionally richer because we have been affected by a Renée Geyer song. She has never taken the soft commercial option. She has remained true to her roots – and in the end we treasure her because, in every note she sings, she tells the truth about human emotions. That is a very special quality and we should love her for letting us share her talent.

BRUCE ELDER

MEET YOU AT JERRY'S

A preface by Ed Nimmervoll

Halfway between Acland Street and the Elwood Beach end of Barkly Street, St Kilda, sits what was once a suburban Melbourne corner shop, still quaintly calling itself Jerry's Milk Bar. Now it's a tiny coffee place and eatery. Amongst the everyday clientele are the musicians, writers and artists who have traditionally congregated in the Elwood/St Kilda area. At the beginning of this project, Renée Geyer lived within walking distance of Jerry's.

We first met to talk about Renée's then forthcoming album, 'Sweet Life'. Around this time she'd been approached by HarperCollins*Publishers* to do her autobiography. One thing led to another, and soon we were meeting regularly at Jerry's in the course of writing this book.

This has not been an easy project for Renée. Although Australia has known her since she was nineteen, we've actually learned very little about Renée the person. Until now, she's always let her music do the talking. She has never been someone to let her personal life be splashed all over the entertainment pages of newspapers and magazines. The more she and I talked, at Jerry's or Renée's house, or the occasional restaurant, the more I realised what a private person Renée is – amazing for someone who has spent most of her life in the public eye.

She's also very honest and open. Having decided to tell her story, she was not going to hold back. From day one this was going to be pure Renée, as the saying goes, no holds barred.

At the same time that Renée dared to venture into her past, I watched her deal with the immediate present – the rollercoaster journey she goes through around the release of an album, the emotional effort poured in and the trauma and pride that follow a record's release. In between were numerous performances, all over the country, Renée always trying new things, challenging herself, her musicians and the songs she'd just recorded. Never taking the easy road.

For me, it was fascinating watching all this from close quarters, seeing how Renée Geyer really does live for her music. For her, life is getting towards the next show and the next record, and making the most of those things when she gets there. Finding time in between to tell her story was sometimes a nuisance, sometimes a welcome distraction.

What we've always known about Renée Geyer is that she's Australia's finest soul singer, and one of the best in the world. When you get close to her, as you will in reading this book, you discover something we've seen more and more of at Renée's live performances in recent years, but maybe not appreciated fully. You realise she's an incredibly witty raconteur. She has a wonderful way with words, and loves to laugh, more often than not at her own expense. She's great company – on and off stage – and has become a good friend.

We still meet at Jerry's for coffee.

Chapter 1

GROWING UP

When I was born my father's first words were, 'Oh, it's only a girl.'

My father is Hungarian, tall, grand, intolerant and very clever academically. Both he and my mother had been through the war. He was strict and unbending in his upbringing of me and my two brothers, Robbie and Dennis. In the fifties, migrants to Australia already had so much to deal with that their children just had to go along with 'The Plan'.

I was born in Melbourne, but from 1956 (when I was three) through to 1966, the main place of my upbringing was the Jewish Migrant Hostel in Greenwich, Sydney. The hostel was run by the Jewish Welfare Society – a big man called Syd Einfeld was the overseer of this project – and it was home to between twelve and fifteen Jewish refugee families. They had all fled war-torn Europe and come to Australia to start again.

My parents managed the hostel. The staff consisted of my mum and dad and various helpers, including the caretaker, Hansie, an old man who used to roam around the building with a broom (I never saw him sweep, but always that broom), and Mrs Goodsell, this adorable, thoroughly Aussie lady who was my mum's right hand in the kitchen. I was never asked to help in the kitchen. My mother knew better than that. I was a definite klutz and I was never ever attracted to cooking – attracted to the end result, but that's it.

In some ways, living in the hostel was a lovely way to grow up. There were always children from different nationalities to play with: Polish, French, Russian, Hungarian. There was lots of playing, and me showing the kids around, but I never really made great friends at the hostel. Maybe my parents didn't want us to get too close, knowing these families wouldn't be there long. My playmates only lived there until their parents got on their feet, so there was a big turnover.

I was always out the back, skipping and playing games on the concrete quadrangle where the clothesline was. We used to play games like 'elastics' and 'sevenies'. When I wasn't in the quadrangle I'd be lying on the big hill leading up to the hostel, reading and singing Beatles songbooks with different friends. Or I'd be stealing empty soft drink bottles for the threepence you could get back on them, or following my brothers around and longing to play soccer with them. They rarely let me, but I always watched from the sidelines on Saturday mornings and helped cut up the oranges at half-time. I thought that was so great. I was always tagging along, making a pest of myself and generally getting in the way.

2

My mother says I was a very curious child, and never happy with a simple answer. My brothers would go away and find out things for themselves, but *I* always had to have everything explained to me. There was a little old man who used to come to visit my parents. He was a hunchback. He used to put me on his knee, and once, my mother tells me, I sat on his lap for half an hour, just looking at him. I wasn't frightened of him. Finally I blurted out, *Where's your neck, and why is your head on your shoulders?* He was really polite and sweet and explained to me that he had had polio when he was little and that this was the result. My mum remembers that I was so sorry for him that I sat there patting his 'head without a neck'.

Another time, one of the fathers of one of the families in the hostel died. As they were carrying him out I insisted on knowing where he was going. They explained that he was dead, that he'd passed away and gone to heaven. *How can he be in heaven?* I was baffled by the thought that anyone could be up there in a sky with no floor. *He's going to fall out!*

I was a very hard child to raise, and very independent from an early age. I always had my own ideas and never liked being told what to do. Because of this I was treated quite harshly by my father. I got smacked a lot; that was his way of dishing out punishment. When I think back to my childhood I don't remember a lot of the good times. The good times usually came from the pretending and the imagining in my little room.

My parents lived in a room we called 'the big room', and I lived in 'the little room' off theirs. My brothers were in another room down the corridor, which was called (guess what?) 'the boys' room'. If I was sick with the flu I'd be allowed to be in the big room all day. I'd lie there and listen to

3

the radio. I could have listened to it all day and night if I was allowed. As soon as I was able to get a transistor radio I slept with it on my pillow.

Some people say prayers before they go to sleep, but in my bedtime ritual, I used to make myself sing ten whole songs that were on the charts at the time or I could not go to sleep. Sometimes I'd get a bit carried away and my father would come in and shout, 'Shut up!' So I'd be under the covers, singing (muffled), *I want to hold your haaaand* ... I *had* to finish my ten songs.

Because the little room was off the big room, if I needed to go to the toilet in the middle of the night I had to wake my parents, much to my father's annoyance, and my mother would have to take me outside. You see, to get to this toilet you had to go out the big room, through the long, dark corridors and out the back door. It was an outside dunny, and a big ordeal. So after a while of being shouted at and dreading the wrath of my father, I just stayed in bed and did my wee-wee there. I was completely awake. *Do it, lie in it, handle it, just don't wake him up. You can explain tomorrow.* They put the mattress out to dry on the hill where everybody drove past. That was my punishment.

My father always used to go on 'The Inventors', a TV show for backyard inventors. I think he won once. At home he was like some mad professor, always building machines of some sort. He invented a thing that made soda water for a cent a bottle, or something. There was also a machine that made records. He made the vinyl, the presser, the whole thing. He had a little shed outside, but sometimes the inventions came into the big room.

By mathematics my father also worked out, based on the odds, how to have a chance of winning the lottery. He had wads and wads of paper with millions of numbers printed on them. It was a project he'd been working on for a long time. I don't know if it was years (when you're little you don't know), *but it was a very long time.* One night my parents went out. A bunch of these papers were resting on the mantelpiece above where the heater was. We were playing ... something happened ... papers fell in the heater ... Next thing there was a fire and the Fire Brigade was there. The hostel wasn't burnt down, but the papers were definitely gone. I was in so much trouble: I wasn't allowed to have presents for the next year. I was very unpopular with my father. In disgrace. He must have thought, 'Why is she here?'

My father was always making something in that shed of his. He made toy soldiers, and invented a game called 'soccer buttons' which my brothers used to play. He made these smooth, dome-shaped buttons which were the soccer team; the ball was a shirt button. You'd play it like tiddlywinks and make the ball jump by squeezing down on the player buttons and hitting the ball button, causing it to slide along the table towards the goals. Chocolate cigarette boxes were the goals on either end. We had a vending machine in the hostel that sold chocolates that came in cigarette packet-shaped boxes. Syd Einfeld, on his numerous visits to the hostel, would always hand out two-shilling pieces to the children, and we used to go straight to that vending machine to get those chocolate ciggies. They came in coloured boxes and my father and my brothers used them for different teams' goals. An entire table surface would be completely buffed and polished to play the game.

My father never took his inventions to a business level. He could have made a fortune, but I don't think he trusted anyone with his 'babies' so he kept his inventions to himself.

Also, I think that once the invention was finished he was not so excited about it any more. His whole thing was the inventing of the invention, the science and the mathematics of making the idea come to life. The minute it was completed, he was ready to move on.

I wanted to learn to play the piano, but my parents never bought one or let me have lessons. They didn't see any future in it. There was an old upright in one of the back rooms of the hostel, and I would go in there at times and try to work out songs that I'd heard on the radio. But I never lasted too long in there, because it was very scary, cold and dark. I always thought that somebody was lurking outside. The hostel had a touch of Miss Havisham's 'Satis House' from *Great Expectations*.

My parents might not have let me have a piano, but they did indulge me with many dolls. I remember Lily, my black doll, and Susie, a white baby doll. Lily, for some unknown reason, had bright red eyes. I was terribly scared of her. My mother would ask, 'Where's Lily?' and I'd say, *Shh, she's sleeping*. She'd always be tucked away in the bottom drawer. Later on, when I was grown up, I would relate this story to my black friends and they would laugh and hint that maybe there was some underlying significance in the fact that Lily, the black doll, was always asleep.

Susie got ravaged. She regularly went to the dolls' hospital to get fixed up. Eventually I loved her to death. I think the same thing happened to my teddy.

When I was a little older I really wanted a life-sized doll. I remember getting Annabelle. She was as big as me. Three weeks later she was outside, left to rust and rot in the elements. The novelty had worn off. *So long, Annabelle …*

My father and I never got on. I don't think he understood me and I really don't think he liked me. It's funny, we were so much alike, but I was much too headstrong for a little girl. He loved me, as a father does, but I was a constant source of annoyance to him. My mother heaped extra love on me because of this. She was always the 'good guy' – emotional, but underneath, very strong. If not for my mother, I don't know what might have happened to me; I couldn't have lived with my father alone – we would have killed each other.

My parents sent my brothers and I to Methodist colleges because they wanted us to get a good education. At that time I don't think there were any Jewish schools up to scratch on an educational level, so they sent me to Ravenswood Methodist Ladies' College, and the boys to Newington College for Boys. Our education must have been a great financial burden on my parents at a time when I'm sure they were really struggling. That's how much it meant to them. Education came first. The Jewishness … they'd deal with that at home.

I was eventually expelled from Ravenswood, for stealing. I used to pinch two-shilling coins from the rich girls' bags. Me and this other girl had this little syndicate going, and because we hadn't been caught we just kept doing it. The way I *did* finally get caught was kinda like a B-grade detective movie. The school, knowing that something was going on but unable to find the culprit, eventually got the police in. They put powder on the money of those girls who were being stolen from all the time. When whoever it was who was doing it washed their hands, their hands would go green. So, throughout the school, detectives went from class to class. When they finally came to mine I was in art class, where there was a tap and sink in the classroom. One by one the detectives would call us up to put our hands under the tap. I remember going up to the sink, dizzy with what I thought I was going to say and what I thought was about to happen to me, dizzy with fright and excitement, perhaps with the thought of getting away with it, but knowing that something definitely important was about to happen. And sure enough, as the water flowed through my fingers, they turned the brightest green you have ever seen. I looked up at the detective and half-heartedly asked, *My green pen?* He just shook his head very slowly, and the whole class was silent. I could feel the heat on my back from the shocked stares. I don't remember what happened to my partner in crime; she wasn't in that art class. We never saw each other again. We were both sent home to our respective families and that was the end of that.

They expelled me. When I got home my dad was sitting there with his head in his hands and my moneybox broken in front of him. He was looking for all this money that he thought I must have squirrelled away. But I wasn't that devious; all I used to do was buy lollies, cream buns and Twisties. My mother always used to make us lunch and never gave us money for school. I'd wanted some of the action from the tuckshop. It was as simple as that.

For what seemed like a long time, months maybe, I remember my life being as if the mute button had been pressed. I remember everything occurring around me and to me, but I don't remember the sounds. Everyone was really quiet.

My parents are so law-abiding, it destroyed them. To be expelled from a private school was like a black mark. My father avoided me, my brothers ignored me and my mother just didn't want to talk about it. The worst part was, my father, who usually gave me and my brothers a good hiding when we were naughty, didn't hit me. That really brought home the seriousness of the whole thing. Not being spoken to I could cope with, but not being hit by him was disturbing to me.

Needless to say, I've never stolen since.

My parents sent me to a psychiatrist. They thought I must have been mentally ill to have done this. I remember asking my father, *Why am I going to the doctor?* He slowly put his newspaper down, looked up and said, 'We're going to see if you're nutty or not,' and back up with the paper. So for a while there I actually thought I was seriously insane. When the results from the psychiatric tests came in, it turned out that I had a really high, university-level IQ. That confounded my father even more, but at least it was the end of the insane theory. If I wasn't nutty then I must have just been plain 'bad'.

From then on, whenever I disobeyed him, instead of being called nutty, I was the 'bad seed'.

They eventually found a new school for me, Willoughby Primary. The headmistress, Mrs Savage, was lovely. She really understood the situation and thought that I'd been given a raw deal. And I think she really liked my mother. So I went there and I was a good girl. *For a while.*

In about 1966 my parents were starting to think about being kosher caterers, because of all the experience my mother had had cooking at the hostel. Eventually they ended up being very successful. But in one of his brainwave nutty-professor moves, my father initially picked Perth, the city in Australia with the least Jews, for them to set up business. I guess he was thinking, 'There are no other kosher caterers, so we'll get all the business! My father went first, and then my mum, my brothers and I followed. Of course, six months later it was all over.

Perth was a very low time in my life. It was the peak of the battles with my father. I was about thirteen, and I very much resented him. It got to the point where my father and I couldn't stand even being in the same room together.

This was one of the contributing factors in my mum leaving my father. She also hated living in Perth, and missed her Sydney family and friends.

So she left my brothers with my father for the moment, and took me back to Sydney where her brother, my uncle Borach, lived. We took a little flat in Dover Heights and she worked at the B'naai Brith, a Jewish function centre, for a while. The flat was small and humble, and my uncle would meet me after school and take me to the kosher restaurant in Woollahra for dinner while my mother worked.

Meanwhile, my father was depressed, and not handling things very well without my mother. He wanted to come back. For my parents to get back together it was very important that my dad and I got along. I wanted it to work out because I knew my mother wasn't happy alone. The family got back together and we moved into a real house in Weonga Road, Dover Heights. The catering business started to thrive and we all lived happily ever ... *Not quite.*

Me and my father? No good. I was now apparently beyond control. I had my own mind and my own thoughts. I felt like I was living with Archie Bunker without the laugh track. The next two years were spent mainly in my room, listening to Dusty Springfield and Aretha Franklin, never eating meals with the family. It was a bad time.

Luckily, though, I had lots of friends at school. Openly I was always the centre of attention – funny, the class clown. We would all do stuff, but I'd be the one who'd made the most noise about it, so I was always the one caught and ultimately sent to the headmistress. That's the way it was all through my high school years. I was in trouble a lot, but I don't think any of my teachers actually disliked me.

My group of girlfriends and I used to laugh a lot. In fact, so much so that I developed a bladder problem. Every time we did something funny or there was hilarious laughter involved, I couldn't seem to hold my bladder. It happened about once a week and I used to have to bring spare sports bloomers with me, just in case. There was a group of about five of us, and they all knew. When this happened, they all had a job to do. *Go team.* One would get me out of there and to the toilets quickly, so I could change. Another one would get newspapers and put them over the puddle. A third girl would put a chair over the newspaper so it couldn't be seen. The remainder would just divert the attention of other people to something else. That emergency bladder team was a finely-tuned machine.

Once there was this announcement over the PA speakers. The headmistress said, 'We want everybody to keep an eye out for the dogs that are coming inside the school. They seem to be leaving puddles everywhere. We're going to have to catch them and put them to sleep.' Being a lover of most animals on earth, I found this *almost* a deterrent, but not quite … it brought on another laughing attack.

But the worst was yet to come. The daughter of one of my parents' best friends was getting married and I was going to be a bridesmaid. I was so excited. But I had a laughing episode at her house once and left a puddle. Her parents said to my parents, 'She's a lovely girl – please don't take this the wrong way – but we don't think that she should be a bridesmaid.' They were afraid that I would leave a puddle under the chuppah at the synagogue. I think that was the last straw for my mother. She decided to take me to Macquarie Street. *Oh-oh!* That's where all the major specialists and surgeons in Sydney were. You only went to Macquarie Street if you had a big problem.

I was taken there by my mother every couple of weeks for I don't know how long. They told me they were shooting a dye up into my bladder that would eventually tighten it. It was done with a syringe inserted right into my urethra. I used to dread it. I'd be nauseous at the thought of having to go. It was an excruciating ordeal to have to go through and, as it turned out, possibly unnecessary, verging on cruel. I found out years later that my problem had been purely psychological and that this was a placebo treatment. It worked, but I don't believe that I should have been subjected to such harsh treatment for something psychological. I was about fourteen or fifteen — very tender years.

Openly I was always someone seeking attention, putting on a show, but inside I was a bit lonely and a little sad. I can't explain this. Maybe it was the shadow of a past life haunting me, or maybe it had something to do with the way I was brought up. I just always felt a loss. When I was a child I really felt it. I didn't know why. I didn't confront it, but it was always there. I certainly never showed it in public. I think my friends would be surprised to know that underneath my bright demeanour I was sad a lot of the time. Being treated the way I was by my father didn't help, either. When you're little, you can only be told you're an idiot so many times before you believe it.

My brothers were both very gifted academically. My father wanted me to do Latin, so I did and I was OK at it. But mathematics didn't interest me at all. Maths was my father's big thing. We used to get smacks from him if we got sums wrong. He had this European method of multiplying and dividing which was very complicated. I was hopeless enough at the English way that I was being taught all day at school, let alone coming home and learning another way. He'd coach us after school – more my brothers than me. They got smacks too.

We didn't get given a lot of encouragement for our achievements; it wasn't my dad's way. He was more about berating us for the things we weren't good at, and I'm sure a lot of my defensiveness came from that.

I left school in the middle of fifth form. I couldn't stand it any more. By this time I was already singing with bands, but the only way my parents would let me leave school was if I went to typing school. They just wanted what they thought was good for me. They were very confused and couldn't just let me leave and be 'nothing'.

The minute I left school my world opened up.

My new lifestyle didn't suit my father. I was constantly fighting with him. He must have thought I was some kind of hooker, because I was always coming home late. He couldn't imagine what I was doing at the hours I was doing it, in jeans in a wine bar, singing, coming home with money. It was very strange behaviour from a nice Jewish teenage girl from Dover Heights.

The time eventually came when there wasn't room in our house for the both of us, and in Weonga Road, he was definitely the boss. I spent years arguing, wrangling, pining to be free, and plotting my revenge. I used to think, *Wait till I get out, he's gonna get it.* When I finally left, I didn't want revenge any more. I was just happy to be free.

Looking back, leaving home was a huge thing to do. A Jewish girl moving out of home at seventeen was unheard of at that time. My mother looks at it now and says, 'Wow, how you did what you did ...!' I didn't think about the enormousness of what I was doing at the time. I just knew I had to get out of there: I couldn't sing in my room, I couldn't come home after ten. I was a grown woman. It was the late sixties and early seventies, and there were all these temptations out there. It wasn't even sex or drugs so much; it was just being independent.

I was out of there.

Jimmy Dodds, the bass player in the group I was in, had a Mini Minor, and in it he came to pick me up to take me away from home. My mother was standing at the door of our house, crying as the Mini Minor drove me away with my dolls – Susie, Lily and Teddy – my Dusty and Aretha records, and my single bed on the roof rack. I just remember driving away and thinking, *Yes!* I was sad, and a little scared, but I knew I had to get out of there. I didn't want to live like my family lived and I didn't want to deal with my father anymore. I knew I had to get away; I was suffocating.

I moved into a flat in Bondi with two other girls and it was a breath of new life. I never looked back.

My mum and I had quite a strong bond, but I had many fights with her too. After I left home, we used to have shouting matches on the phone. One next-door neighbour I met at a party years later said to me, 'We used to hear you shouting at your poor mother.' *You didn't hear how loud my mother was shouting back at me on the other end!* (I grew up in a family that shouted at each other. That's how we communicated.) I guess I was rude and impatient with my mother because subconsciously I wanted to eliminate any chance of going back home and living with my parents again. Not that they wanted me back; I'm sure they were very relieved.

We've come through a lot of that now. It's amazing what the grace and wisdom of age can do to people. I think there's still a part of my father that doesn't approve of what I do, but there's the major part that's very proud. My father's way is not to tell me to my face that I'm great but he'll tell everybody else.

He's always been a Mahler man, which immediately makes him *not* a fan of pop music. We were always listening to Mahler or some such dark music through my childhood. Very beautiful, but very depressing. We always had to be quiet around the house when it was on. My music is not his cup of tea, but he thinks I'm one of the best at doing it. His attitude is, 'Of all the shit music out there, my daughter's shit music is the best.' I am thankful for the compliment.

All in all I love my parents very much. I especially love my mummy – I'd be lost without her. There's rarely a day that goes by that I don't call her.

I think I'd be in a mental asylum if I wasn't a singer. If I didn't have the personality I have, and if I'd lived the life that I was expected to, I think I'd be a really sad, sorry, grey person. Or I'd be married to some unhappy man and have unhappy children around me.

There's a word in German, '*ubermutig*'. It sort of means over-excited, or acting up. My parents applied it to me when I was young, as a response to my showing off, wanting to be the centre of attention, or generally just being too frisky for my own good. As long as I remember I was always *ubermutig*, and now I make a living out of it.

I appreciate my parents' strengths, and I guess, I've inherited that from them. It's enabled me to be in this career of music and prevail through the hard times. They did the best they could, raising a very unusually independent and stubborn little girl at a time when there were no guide books or talk shows addressing this problem. I think, finally, they understand me and love me as I am and I am so thankful for that.

In the end I wouldn't change a thing.

Chapter 2

JEWISHNESS

My name comes from the time of my mother's internment at Auschwitz. Her parents and her sister, who had three small children, were all put to death in the gas chambers. At some point the inmates of that notorious concentration camp were lined up and put into two queues: those who were young and fit enough to work, and those who were too young, too old or too ill. In the same queue as my mother was a girl from her village. My grandmother's last words to my mother were, 'Stay with Renée.' She did. Renée, along with my mother, survived. When I was born I was given her name.

My mother and her family had been driven out of their town of Bratislava in Czechoslovakia in 1942 when she was sixteen years of age. She hid for two years and, when finally captured, was interned from 1944 to 1945. After a horrifying stint in

Auschwitz she was transferred to the camp in Mauthausen in Austria. This was where she was finally liberated.

My father, meanwhile, had fled Hungary for Palestine in 1939, sensing what was to come. For the next four years he did odd jobs, but by the time my mother arrived in 1945 on one of the 'exodus' ships, he was well established and was managing a canteen run by the British. My mother and father fell in love and were married. They returned to Budapest, my father's home, where my big brother Dennis was born. The family then moved to Paris in 1949, and here they finally made a decision about where to live for the rest of their lives. There were three choices for Eastern Europeans after the war: the United States, Canada or Australia. In Palestine, my father had met Aussie diggers. He liked their honest, easygoing attitudes, so he decided he wanted to go to the place where they came from. The family waited two years for their permit. In 1951 they finally arrived in Australia.

My brother Robert was born in 1952. Then, on 11 September 1953, I was born: Renée Rebecca Geyer.

In 1992 The Sydney Jewish Museum opened in Darlinghurst, Sydney. At the time, this was the only museum in the world which used as its guides survivors of the holocaust. My mother volunteered for a position. It was a very therapeutic experience for her. She struggled, as she still does, with her memories, but her visits to the museum were good for her. Even more healing was Steven Speilberg's 'Schindler's List'. The openness that that movie brought to the subject of the holocaust really helped many Jews, including my mother, face their traumas. Speilberg didn't stop his truth-telling mission after making the movie, either. He sent a film crew all around the world, interviewing every single survivor who could or would talk about his or her experiences during the holocaust.

My mother was one of those interviewed. She's always said that the holocaust wasn't something that should be thrown in people's faces, but that, on the other hand, it should never be forgotten. It's hard to comprehend, but there are still people in the world who deny that the holocaust ever occurred, or that its atrocities occurred to the extent that they did. I lived with someone who went through it, so the truth is vivid in my mind. Those one-on-one interviews are in the Washington archives as evidence of this truth, and as an assurance that the survivors' stories will never be forgotten.

Mum always used to half look, and half not look, at every documentary on the holocaust, to see if she could see herself in the footage. In the camps she used to carry a clean white hessian bandanna with her. If ever she was put in a line-up, she wanted to cover her shaved head and look presentable, so she would always wear this piece of cloth as a scarf. Ever after, Mum was always looking for this white-scarved head in photos and footage from those days. Then, one day recently, someone sent her a big book of photographs of the liberation of all the main concentration camps. In this book, in the section on Mauthausen, she saw a picture with a little white dot in amongst the crowd. Something made my mother have that picture enlarged. And there she was: my mother, skinnier than I've ever seen her. It was so amazing to see. She's got it on the wall at home.

My mother has never been a bitter person. To have been a six-stone teenager walking over dead bodies, escaping death day after day – to have gone through that and not be bitter and twisted, is pretty amazing. She has suffered a lot, and she has some emotional problems, but on the whole she's come through it all with quite a balanced view of everything, and a lot of dignity.

Funnily enough, I didn't learn anything of my mother's experiences till I was nearly grown up. She never talked about it when I was little. We were discouraged from watching TV shows like 'Hogan's Heroes' at home. That was my first inkling that there was something wrong. There was a little bit of an explanation from my parents, but not much. Any further questioning unleashed hysteria, so I left it alone. Whatever it was my mother had experienced, it was obviously too horrible to contemplate.

Most of the males in my mother and father's family were rabbis or cantors. My parents have always upheld strong Jewish traditions throughout my upbringing. They were kosher caterers and kept a kosher kitchen in our house. When I was a young girl, I went to all the services on high holidays and performed all the religious duties my parents wanted me to do. I did these things more out of a sense of duty than any understanding of what was going on. I didn't mind the traditions so much. I just didn't believe in my heart that all the strict rules relating to the high holidays (Yom Kippur, Rosh Hashanah and Passover) were something I would stick to when I grew up. I decided pretty early in my life that I was quite happy and proud to be Jewish, but that I didn't relate to going to the temple and praying about it, and generally suffering (as in Yom Kippur when we had to fast for a day to repent our sins) because of it.

Women are considered quite secondary in most synagogues. Except in the liberal synagogues, women are seated well apart from the men. When I was little, there was nothing in Judaism for me to latch on to. It was very much a man's religion. There were no great stories about girls in the Bible – nothing to take an example from.

Jewishness was more important to my brothers. They both had very elaborate Bar Mitzvahs (the ceremony marking a boy's attainment of manhood at the age of thirteen). I never had a Bat Mitzvah (the girl's equivalent), because my mother never had one. At least, that's the reason given to me ... For months and months my brothers had to learn Hebrew prayers to sing and recite for their Bar Mitzvahs. I sat on the sidelines, envious of the attention. I *so* wanted a Bat Mitzvah. I wanted it for the occasion, the gifts, and, most of all, the party!

I joined a Zionist group there for a minute, like all Jewish teenagers did. I liked it for the games, the camping and the adventure stuff, but wasn't interested in the rhetoric – the 'getting Jerusalem back at all costs' stuff. It was very militant.

My parents tried, like all normal Jewish parents, to keep me and my brothers socially within the Jewish community. This became difficult when they sent us to schools that were predominantly Christian.

Growing up in Sydney, I never felt all that different from my friends because of my Jewishness. I was more self-conscious about the fact that my parents were foreigners. Their accents were a bit embarrassing, and I used to wish I could go somewhere and have steak and chips like 'normal' kids, instead of schnitzels and gefilte fish, which I now love.

I hung out with Jewish people most when my mother and I came back from Perth and she enrolled me in Dover Heights High School. Dover Heights was full of Jewish girls.

There was a group of us: Rita, a second-generation Russian Jew, Roberta, a Sri Lankan Jew, and Nilly, an Israeli. There was also Jane, an English girl, who we regarded as an honorary Jew. This was my team and throughout high school we were the best of friends. They're all married now, with children. Some are divorced. I don't see them, but I hear about them from time to time.

After travelling all over the world, and now settling back here in Australia, I find it heart-warming to run into the 'new' generation of Jewish people. Not only do they have the easygoing Aussie sense of humour that my father loved all the way back in Palestine, but they are still so very Jewish. It's a lovely hybrid that didn't exist when I was young. I feel a real affinity with these people.

The Jews are a formidable race, one of the most ancient tribes on the planet. The way they talk, their logic, their humour – these are very distinctive things. You can meet a Jew from Paris or a Jew from Sydney and know that they're from the same tribe. They might not go to synagogue, but you know they're Jewish from the way they are. Whereas you can meet a Catholic person and not necessarily know they're Catholic, most of the time you can pick a Jew. Not by their looks, but by their way.

My Jewishness radiates from me without my even being aware of it. Because it's not so much a religion as a race of people, I can't help but feel Jewish. I'm proud, and I respect my race. I don't think I'd be doing what I do so well, and for so long, if not for my Jewishness.

Chapter 3

THE LADDER OF BANDSVILLE

Joining a band was not the easy way to make a mark in the music business, but it was my way.

At all the dances I went to there were always bands performing, not solo artists. I'd been watching music shows on Saturday-morning TV – shows like 'Uptight' and 'Happening 70' – and in my head, in my own little world, I saw myself being able to sing better than the girl from Flake or the girl from Aesop's Fables. I *really* wanted to be in a band. I just knew I could do it. I loved bands because they seemed so in control, like they were in a world of their own. It seemed like the coolest thing to do. I imagined the fantastic life they must have been having.

I used to read all the music magazines, and *Go-Set* was the rock bible at that time. One day in 1968 I looked up the agency that managed Flake and Aesop's Fables and other groups with girl lead singers, and I caught the 381 bus from Weonga Road, Dover Heights, all the way to Railway Square in Sydney. I wore the dress I had to beg my mother to buy for me for dances, a very vampish crossover black crepe number from Merivale and Mr John, which was *the* hip shop in those days. I thought I looked very grown-up. I was fifteen.

I got to the agency and was asked to sit in reception. There were posters of all the artists of the time, including Wendy Saddington, Chain, Spectrum, and a group called Gutbucket who I loved. There were all these groovy-looking people in the office. I was thrilled. I thought, *Wow, if I don't get a job as a singer, maybe I'll work here as a receptionist!*

It seemed forever, but finally I was ushered into an office. I can't remember the man's name, nor his face. I must have blocked them out. I walked in and said, *I'm a really good singer and I want to join a band.* He just looked at me, waiting for my next statement. In the end he was dismissive and patronising, and I don't blame him. Who was I? Just some kid. I had no tapes, I had nothing. I just expected to walk in and be told what the next step would be. I remember leaving the agency very pissed off. The guy hadn't even heard me sing! He obviously didn't realise what a big thing it was for me to come from Dover Heights to Railway Square on a bus, in a black crepe crossover dress, in the school holidays, without my parents knowing.

My dream to join a band finally came true when my best friend at the time suggested that I audition for her friends' band. Apart from my parents, who'd heard me sing around the house and hadn't thought anything of it, this friend was the only one who really knew I could sing. I remember singing Led Zeppelin riffs with her – *Doo doo doo doo do do do do do doo do … Living. Loving. Just like a woman.* She was the only one who knew my secret ambition.

She was also my first real rebel friend. We smoked marijuana together. We used to take about ten diet pills at a time and think we were on speed. We would sit on the south end of Bondi Beach and watch the surfers. Both being Jewish girls, hanging out with a non-Jewish crowd meant we were very rebellious for our time.

Anyway, she had these friends who had an after-school band at Sydney High. They used to do yacht clubs and private parties. She told me they were looking for a singer and, after much coaxing from her, I went along to one of their rehearsals. The audition was at one of the boys' very sumptuous houses in Sydney's eastern suburbs. In the rumpus room. For some reason I'd always longed for a rumpus room. All my friends had rumpus rooms, and this was a deluxe rumpus room.

The band, all very young, spoilt and good-looking, were kind of ignoring us when we arrived, acting all immersed in some two-chord masterpiece they were backbreakingly trying to learn. I was impressed – but then, I was thrilled *anywhere* a band was playing. I waited, knowing I was about to be asked to sing. I remember being nervous but not worried. They finished playing the song and asked me what I wanted to sing, reeling off the names of famous songs of the day, like 'Season of the Witch', 'House of the Rising Sun' and 'G.L.O.R.I.A.'. I picked the Bee Gees' song 'To Love Somebody'.

When I sang the first line I immediately knew I was surprising these guys, as well as myself. Something great was happening. This wasn't the dull sound of my voice in

25

my parents' carpeted living room, singing into a hairbrush. This was the very grown-up and echoey tone of a lead singer in a band.

All of a sudden these boys changed from really cool eastern-suburbs Great Danes into enthusiastic, yapping Labrador puppies, eager to know when I could join. *That was it*. I knew straightaway that it was the end of my life as I knew it … music took over my life and I never looked back.

The first gig was about two weekends later at a private party. It was late 1969. We played Spencer Davis, Cream, Moody Blues and Janis Joplin songs; never any of the black stuff I was listening to at home. Aretha Franklin was still some untouchable sound that I would listen to in my bedroom at night and didn't want to mess with at mere mortal gigs.

We did more rehearsals then than I ever do now. We were seventeen years old. Gigs were hard to come by, so rehearsals *were* our gigs. We'd try out new songs and people would come and hear us. I wasn't always crazy about the songs I sang with this band, but I don't recall arguing with them about it. At this point I was just happy to be in a band; I would have sung 'Mammy' if they'd asked me. My attitude was, *Give me anything and I'll show you I can sing it*. Anyway, the band were in charge. And they had *instruments*! I didn't realise until later that they were actually not very good musicians – just rich boys who had equipment.

Through that band I met Jim Dodds, a bass player who was constantly in my ear coaxing me to move on. This was the beginning of a pattern: someone, usually a musician, pulling me out of one band and taking me to the next. I left that first band, which was little more than a hobby for those boys, and joined a better band with Jimmy. It was called Dry Red.

With better musicians, I started getting serious gigs. It was early 1970. Performing at the Kask, a wine bar in Bondi, was an important turning point for me. We used to get five bucks a night. I couldn't believe it: I was starting to get paid for this! The Kask was a surfie bar. What I remember most about it is the smell of cigarettes, the taste of Cinzano and coke, and the strains of Iron Butterfly's 'In-A-Gadda-Da-Vidda' playing in the background. The place was always full of Adonis-like surfies with nicknames like Terry T-Shirt, Donald Duck and Astro Boy. It was very bohemian for a young, middle-class Jewish girl like me. I loved it. I think the Kask is a Kentucky Fried Chicken place now.

People remind me that when they first came to hear me sing in Dry Red I had my back to the audience, singing to the band. They thought it was part of the act, but that couldn't have been further from the truth: I was so nervous. I hadn't yet become an entertainer and I didn't care if people didn't see my face; I couldn't bear people staring at me. My showmanship level hadn't yet come up to par with my vocal abilities. But even though my back was turned, my voice was always loud and clear.

I never used to wear much make-up, just the odd bit of mascara. (This wasn't Shirley Bassey.) My parents couldn't understand this – couldn't understand that I was going out to perform in a pair of jeans and a T-shirt, with no make-up; and that I was calling myself a singer.

They thought this singing thing would be a passing fancy ... something I'd get over. But with Dry Red I was doing wine bars and coming home late on school nights, and now they were getting worried. This was when they finally let me leave school on the condition that I go to typing school.

By now things were getting pretty bad at home with me and my father, so when I finally made the decision to leave, Jimmy Dodds, having moved me out of my first band, helped me move out of home and into a flat in Bondi with a couple of girls that I'd met at the Kask. When I moved to Bondi, Jim was always around. Some boys are like really good girlfriends. Jim was really funny and good company, and all the girls loved him. I'm not sure whether he was a really good bass player – I can't remember that – but he's not in the business now, so maybe he wasn't. But Jim was my first musician friend. He had a wicked sense of humour. This became a prerequisite for friendships for me all through my life.

I thought Dry Red was *it*. The guitarist was Eric McCusker (later of Mondo Rock), and the keyboard player was a guy called Vic Nicholson – very talented, bordering on a genius. I was in awe of Vic. We had a couple of drummers – Billy Lansdowne, a surfer, and then Greg Tooey. Dry Red rehearsed in Eric McCusker's garage in Tamarama, just south of Bondi.

We were doing Spencer Davis Group songs at the time – *'I'm a man, yes I am, and I can't help but love you so.'* I remember people saying, 'You can't sing that song, you're a woman.' That never worried me. We were also doing Julie Driscoll. I liked Julie Driscoll more than Janis Joplin. Driscoll was more interesting to me. It was white music and I enjoyed it, but inside I still had a hankering for the black stuff. I was still going home to Aretha.

A major turning point in the life of that band came when Vic Nicholson had to leave and a piano player called George Almanza joined the group. Jimmy Dodds had left by now, and George became my new soul mate and partner in crime. We connected immediately. It was quite a flirty relationship in the beginning, but it never went beyond that. George and I hung out in our own little world.

In late 1971, we both auditioned for and then joined a jazz-rock band called Sun. I was moving from better band to better band. Sun had already done some major gigs and had been written up in *Go-Set*. While they were still pretty much unknown, to George and I, from where Dry Red was, it was the big league.

Sun was into avant-garde people like Sun Ra, John Coltrane, Theloneus Monk and Miles Davis. The band's aims were true, but I always thought we were just a little inexperienced to be playing this sort of music. The boys were completely genuine in their love for that music, but it was a little silly to think that as a young band we were going to be able to play that way and know what we were doing. John Coltrane and Miles Davis, to get where they got, went through the basic bebop phase first, and it took a lot of years of playing with different people to get to the amazing place where they ended up. Sun wanted to go straight there. It's very easy for a musician to just start improvising and going nuts all around the scale and think it's brilliant, but there was method to the 'madness' of guys like Miles Davis and Coltrane, which is why very few people can mimic that stuff. A lot of musicians are so into the idea of jazz and the technique of it that they completely miss the point and disappear up their own bumholes. Sun was that way. But it was a priceless training ground for me. To be seventeen years old and learning about all these people – Coltrane, Miles, Cecil Taylor, Elvin Jones, Leon Thomas (the warbler), Theloneus Monk, Pharaoh Sanders and Jimi Hendrix – was quite incredible and to this day has left me with a deep appreciation for this music.

The bandleader of Sun was Keith Shadwick, the sax player. He was the culprit of all the seriousness. I thought he was brilliant until I heard the real Coltrane, and the 'early' Coltrane. Then it dawned on me: Keith Shadwick was very good at 'doing' Coltrane. He understood Coltrane in a theoretical way, like a journalist would analyse and understand a musician. He was the one who turned us all onto that amazing music, but I think he was actually the one amongst us with the least musical talent. I believe he has a shop in London now where he sells books about that sort of music.

The bass player, Henry Corey, was a sweetheart – an Italian boy, plump, cuddly and very hairy; always polite and making peace. He'd pick me up for gigs and generally look after me. He was musically capable of handling what Sun was dishing out, but he was a traditionalist as well.

We had a guitar player from America, Chris Sonnenberg. Chris was a really good guitarist, but always had his 'effect' pedal on. It made a normally straight note 'wobbly'-sounding. It used to make his guitar sound like what jelly looks like when you carry it on a plate. I always used to wish that somehow he would break that pedal. To this day I have 'pedal phobia'. Chris Sonnenberg was a bluesman, but he did go 'out there' musically with the rest of us. I liked him, but again, I didn't have as much in common with him as with my Georgie boy.

The drummer was Gary Norwell, a fragile, very neurotic character. I think back now and wonder how I never went crazy with his kind of drumming. I never knew where 'one' was.

Let me explain.

The classic beat of most songs is based on four beats to the bar – *everything* is based on that. 'One' is the first beat of the four. If a drummer's going to play against that beat and mess with the time signature, he really has to know what he's doing. The great thing about messing with that beat is knowing exactly where those four beats are, playing against it and around it, but always landing back on it. You've got to know where 'one' is if you're going to play all over the joint. The beauty of a great solid beat is that the front line can play off it, knowing that they have this bedrock underneath them. At least, that's the way it is in rhythm and blues. In jazz you don't have to rely on the four beats to the bar, but you still have to know where those four beats are, instinctively.

Gary used to play with the beat and lose it. Imagine what that used to do to the rest of the band! With Sun there was never any solid ground. It was like walking on moving earth. I was constantly looking around asking, *Where's 'one'?* Gary couldn't tell me – he didn't know. What with no solid beat, the jelly on the plate, and a front line in constant confusion? *Very avant-garde!*

We paid for our lack of knowing where 'one' was. Sun eventually got sacked from Chequers, a club in Sydney, because the audience was so confused that no-one could dance to us.

The band then started performing at a place called the Arts Factory in the heart of Sydney. It was a hippy kind of place and had LSD Fog lighting. LSD Fog was a famous company at the time that specialised in lighting to mess with your head. In those days the lightshows were as important as the music – a trip in themselves. The better clubs had the better lightshows.

At the Arts Factory the audience would lie on cushions, marijuana'd out of their brains, and gaze at the lights and the parachute ceiling. It was a common sight to see people just sitting there, mesmerised by what was going on around them, as opposed to wanting to dance. We didn't get many gigs like this but we adored them; they were like concerts. *These* audiences didn't care where 'one' was. (In fact, I'm sure they had their own ideas.)

It was around this time that my mother bought me my first PA, a 60-watt Yamaha, from a shop in Kent Street. It was tiny for a band playing big venues. Thinking back now, it was just a big stereo, but I was very excited to get it. We used it once, the first time we did the Arts Factory, and it was stolen. That was my first lesson in rock'n'roll: *never buy your own PA.*

Another lesson I learned during those Art Factory days was how to treat support bands. I'll never forget the people we supported when I was in these early bands and who were kind to us. It meant so much when the headline band acknowledged us, introduced themselves and shook our hands. If, on top of that, they actually liked what we did, then that was an added bonus. I have a lot of respect for Mike Rudd and Bill Putt from Spectrum, and the La De Das – Keith Barber, Phil Keys and Kevin Borich. They were two of the bands we worked with a lot in those days who were always so supportive. When you think that no-one else gives a shit, but then someone who you think is really great does, it's very inspiring.

When we did the big gigs I was always in awe of the main bands with their roadies loading in the equipment. Sun didn't have a roadie – just a friend, Greg, who used to help us, and who was far too skinny and delicate to be carrying all those boxes. I always felt so sorry for him. Next to Greg, the roadies from those other bands always looked mighty good.

It was a very adventurous time for me, musically. I loved to reinterpret songs my own way. In Sun there were hardly any real songs in a traditional sense. Instead there was scatting, making noises and improvisation. I now know that it's great for a singer to start with that sort of training. Whenever I go out and do what I do in front of strangers, I'm aware that that background has helped me in terms of my lack of inhibition.

Sun was happy that they had an uninhibited singer who was willing, musically, to try anything on. I loved the fact that we were playing original music at a time when most bands did mainly 'covers'.

Horst Leopold was our manager. He was German, with a very thick accent, and fond of going around saying, 'This band Sun is *grrrrooving* their arrrse off.' Horst used to smoke these really heavy cigarettes – Gitane or Gaulois – and he had a terrace house in Paddington with a great art and record collection. I discovered most of the jazz that I love through Sun and through him. He was very exotic, and maybe just a tad sinister, which in a way was kind of attractive to me. He was a jazz aficionado, which he still is today, and he now runs a club in New York called Sweet Basils where all the leading jazz artists play.

Horst was the one who got the RCA contract for us. We did an album called 'Sun '72' at Copperfield Studio in Sussex Street, Sydney. Making that album was an odd experience. I remember being really impatient, wanting to get my bit down on tape and it taking forever to get to that point. For a band that was into spontaneity and improvisation, this was a most *un*spontaneous procedure. But the prospect of making my first record was exciting. There were a few arguments here and there, but we ended up agreeing and just picking the strongest songs from our set, all original. The album was basically Keith Shadwick's baby. I was proud, even though it wasn't particularly my kind of music.

I think I might have been a meal ticket for Sun at that time. This big, blonde, busty girl with bare feet, a big voice and a strange demeanour might have been quite compelling to audiences in those days. Roger Davies, who went on to become one of the biggest managers in the world, was then a writer for the *Daily Planet*. I remember he wrote a piece about how I sang, and about how I looked like some Greek goddess up there – motionless but riveting. I thought it was funny when I read it; I didn't see myself in that way – I was just very self-conscious. That was my first review.

The band must have known I was important in getting them attention and gigs. It was when I joined that Sun started getting more press coverage, like appearing on the ABC TV program 'GTK' and 'Radio with Pictures'. Keith Shadwick ended up sacking me and George. He didn't think we were taking things seriously enough – we seemed to be playing and singing in our own world.

It was true: George and I used to have our own code of communication … a look here, a wink there. I guess on the night of the sacking there must have been extra looks and extra winks, because Keith thought we'd been smoking joints. Smoking wasn't our problem; boredom was. In Sun, everyone was too serious about being serious about the playing of their instruments, instead of just letting nature take its course. With Keith and Gary, music wasn't second nature to them. Anyhow, George's and my apparent non-seriousness was our undoing.

I was devastated when I was sacked, more from the blow to my ego than anything else, but I had acquired enough of a name in my own right to move on. In my heart what I really wanted to do was soul music. I was headed for anything that sounded funky. After Sun I was longing to be in a band with songs, with words, and with a drummer who knew where 'one' was.

The nightclub scene was amazing in Sydney in the late sixties and early seventies, thanks to the American Vietnam servicemen coming to Australia for R&R. Boats would dock at Potts Point and all these soldiers and marines would swarm through Kings Cross and Sydney in general. A lot of black entertainers from that era came here and ended up staying. It was an exciting time. It meant there were a lot of what were called showbands, soul and R'n'B revue bands. That scene kept a lot of Sydney musicians in regular work.

In late 1972 I auditioned for the resident band at Jonathans, a fancy nightclub in the heart of Sydney. This was one of the big clubs, up there with Whisky-A-Go-Go and Chequers. It was one of those places I'd heard about as a schoolkid but had never been allowed to go to. And here I was, auditioning to be in their house band! *That was big.* Each member of the band got sixty bucks a week! *Wow.* As a receptionist, you could only get about thirty-five to forty dollars a week at my age.

I found out later that Harry Brus, who plays bass with me today, was at that audition.

Harry, I have to say, is like Zelig, the character in the Woody Allen movie who pops up everywhere – with Hitler, Mussolini, Roosevelt, with Marilyn Monroe, at the signing of the US Constitution ... he's everywhere. You just see his head. Harry's like that. I've found out that he's been at most of the major musical events in my life. He was in that resident band at Jonathons and at the club that day, watching.

At the audition the owner of the club, John Spooner, was in the audience section of the club. He had a microphone. 'OK, sing,' he said. So I sang. Then he said, 'Sing that again without the vibrato.' (Vibrato is the wavering of a voice when a singer holds a note. Some people have big ones, like Dusty Springfield. Other people have very fast ones, like Randy Crawford or even our very own Deni Hines. I guess mine is just an average kind of vibrato.) So I sang the song again with what I thought was less vibrato, but it must have sounded the same to Mr Spooner (as he liked to be called), because I didn't get the job. I thought it funny that Bobbie Marchini, the girl with the fastest vibrato this side of the black stump, did.

Not long after this I auditioned for Nine Stage Horizon, the resident band playing at the Oceanic in the Coogee Bay Hotel. They were a covers band but were made up of really well-known session musicians. They were the first band I'd heard that were really tight ... and they played black music. I got *that* job.

The guitar player in that nine-piece band was so talented. His name was Mark Punch. Mark and his brother Phil single-handedly turned me onto the music that would shape me for the rest of my life. I already had Aretha, but they gave me Donnie Hathaway, BB King, Freddie King, Albert King, John Lee Hooker, Bill Withers, Muddy Waters, even Marty Robbins and George Jones. They turned me onto the beauty of the soulful voice, whatever the style of music.

I was also discovering my own new music: Gladys Knight, and Laura Lee, this great black singer who had an album out called 'Women's Love Rights'. She sounded like Rod Stewart before Rod Stewart. I also loved Merry Clayton and Thelma Houston's Jimmy Webb-written 'Sunshower' album. I met Thelma many years later and asked her about it. All she said was, 'Oh that.' I was shattered.

When I joined Nine Stage Horizon, which was essentially a showband, some people thought I'd sold out. But I'd never had so much fun as I had singing the songs I sang in that band. That material gave me so much more pleasure than Sun's ever did.

Then, just like I'd done with Jimmy Dodds and George Almanza before, I left Nine Stage Horizon, this time with March Punch. We formed Mother Earth, and Harry Brus joined us on bass soon after.

Mother Earth's drummer, Russell Dunlop, who also joined us around this time, was a really happy-go-lucky kind of guy. He had an unbeatable knack of laying down *the* incredible groove. He was a great funk drummer. (This boy really knew where 'one' was.) Then there was Jim Kelly, who joined us later as second guitar player. Jim was a fine player, more sweet and technical than Mark Punch, who was a gutsy rhythm and soul kind of player; real chicken-pluckin'.

Mother Earth was the toast of the musical town. Everyone was coming to our gigs. The band even took me back to Melbourne for the first time since I was a baby. The Melbourne music scene was so cool compared to Sydney. Because of the R&R sailors, Sydney, especially Kings Cross, was very nightclub-oriented; lots of gold chains and cover bands. The showband mentality was everywhere. Melbourne, at least the Melbourne *we* experienced, was more original and creative.

Mother Earth did a week-long tour of two or three gigs a night. We had just one roadie with a truck, and when we finished one gig he would pack up, go ahead to the next gig and we'd meet up with him there. The last gig of the night was always something like Berties or the T.F.Much Ballroom, Melbourne's equivalent to the Arts Factory. It was amazing how many of those places there were in Melbourne – spaces that had been turned into music venues. There were clubs too, but they weren't RSL-type clubs like in Sydney. To me it seemed the Melbourne scene was more joint than alcohol oriented – more musical and mellow.

Mother Earth was very much a Sydney soul band. We must have looked so show biz. Russell Dunlop always made sure I wore evening dresses. I remember wanting to hang out with Harry Brus during the break at one of those late-night psychedelic gigs, but he kept avoiding me, not wanting to stand near me because of my silly outfit.

In the days of Mother Earth, soul music was generally considered middle-of-the-road here in Australia, except by those people who loved it. But people, after hearing it, would usually be converted. I guess it was almost like children who have been forced by their parents to be vegetarians and then are given a bit of a burger by someone: their eyes light up and they go mad. We were the burger. At that time there really weren't any of our type in Melbourne. We had enough of that musical coolness and originality to fit in with Melbourne, but we *were* a soul band. We put on a show, as well as played great music.

Mother Earth didn't end up with much money after that first week in Melbourne. Having caught a train down, Harry

Brus and I blew our money on airfares back. We ended up with just twelve dollars each, but I didn't care. I'd had my first grown-up aeroplane ride. Very exciting.

In 1973 I made my first record with RCA as a solo artist. Horst Leopold got me a solo record deal, but I wanted Mother Earth with me, to keep the sound that we had. I was very much a band singer.

We recorded the album at Col Joye's studio on Glebe Point Road. We did the recording in the day and gigged at night. The producer, Gus McNeil, used to pick me up on his motorbike from Paddington each morning and take me to the studio. The record company A&R man, Rocky Thomas, was this big old guy who drank a lot. Every morning when I got into the studio he'd ask, 'How can you look so good so early?' *Because I'm twenty and you're not!*

The record was called 'Renée Geyer'. When I listen to it now I think it's pretty corny, but the band sounds good. Other than the fact that I could sing the songs the way I wanted, I wasn't really in a position to tell people what songs to put on an album in those days. There was some schmaltzy stuff on there, but I didn't realise that till much later. (It wasn't until 'Ready to Deal' that I became a bit more sure of what I wanted to do.) The record, released in 1973, wasn't hugely successful, but it did help my profile. I started to be talked about. I was beginning to do TV shows on my own and was appearing with other bands as a special guest. Once, it was with the great keyboard player Bobby Gebert. We used to do gigs in this curry house. People would be eating while we were playing; I hated that. But the music was always really good. Bobby Gebert still is an incredible musician. Now there's a wicked boy …!

It wasn't until 'It's a Man's Man's World' came out in 1974 that tails really started wagging.

Mother Earth split up in late 1973. There was never a real moment of it happening; we just all sort of moved on. This was the start of my solo career. Throughout those band years I never was of the opinion, *Oh, I'm going to leave and go solo and be big*. It was more, *I'll never leave unless I can find a better band*. That might sound mercenary, but it's a good musician's way. You can only be as great as the people around you let you be, or push you to be. I wanted to move up the ladder of bandsville, and hopefully bandsville would lead me to starsville ...

I love interacting with great musicians and making music. If it's the right combination, there's nothing like it. I started out in bands, and to this day I consider the band as much the show as I am. Sure, people come to hear me sing, but the musicians are so much a part of what I do. Musicians don't back me, they are alongside of me. They paint the picture with me. I think that's what makes for a really good evening. What keeps me going is the exhilaration and love of the way my voice sounds with a certain group of people – as if it's coming out of some magical speaker.

As a singer I made an impression. From the very first time I opened my mouth and sang to those boys in that rumpus room, right up until now, it's been the same – I impress people with my voice. There's never been a time that I haven't, and that's the truth. In everything else I've been mediocre, but in that one thing I've always been very consistent. In a way, it's weird going through life knowing that this is the one thing you do that comes from the heart and is so pure and so important to you that if you lost it, you'd almost feel like you'd lose life itself.

Anyway, I'm happy to say that I'm still playing with the best musicians around.

Oh, and now I *usually* know where 'one' is.

Chapter 4

READY TO DEAL IN A MAN'S WORLD

My twenty-first birthday party at the Bondi Lifesaver, a club in Sydney, was also my farewell party. I was about to be flown to Melbourne by RCA to record my second album, 'It's a Man's Man's World'.

After Mother Earth fizzled out I had ended up doing a residency at the Bondi Lifesaver with some of the musicians from Mother Earth, but under the name Renée Geyer Band. This was the beginning of solosville for me. We'd play before all the big bands came on. One night Billy Thorpe played and was so loud he killed the fish in the big tank in the middle of the room. The cleaners came in the next day and there they were ... deadskie.

It was a great party. My mother did the catering, and there

were about a hundred people there that night – all my Sydney band, along with Ricky May, Billy ('fish-killer') Thorpe, and assorted friends from my childhood years – all chowing down on gigantic turkey legs, smoked salmon, caviar and pavlovas. As a birthday present my band all chipped in to buy me luggage for my Melbourne trip.

In preparation for recording 'It's a Man's Man's World', RCA sat me in a room and let me pour over their catalogue of black music to pick songs for the album. I just thought, *Wow, I'm in hog heaven!* I could pick anything I wanted – from the Temptations to James Brown to New Birth to Dusty Springfield. In those days, local material was rarely pitched to solo artists unless the artist sought it. In my case, because of my absolute obsession with black music, it made the chance that I'd be pitched something I'd like from an Australian writer even more remote. Besides, I have to admit that I loved the idea of singing the kind of music that I listened to at home every night, and doing covers was not such a no-no in those days. (I did steer clear of Aretha, though; some things are sacred, and I'd already made that mistake on my previous album with 'Do Right Woman'.)

Tweed Harris was employed to produce 'It's a Man's Man's World'. Tweed had been with The Groove, and more recently had produced Sherbet. He was a great arranger, and perhaps producer, but not very original. Tweed would copy the arrangements of the songs I picked almost exactly (just like karioke). Not that I minded; in my naiveté I thought that only the singing mattered, and that I'd make the songs my own by putting my vocal stamp on them. In a way, that's what ended up happening, especially with 'Man's World'.

Ian ('Molly') Meldrum came to the sessions at Armstrong Studios in Melbourne. Everybody was so excited about him being there, even back then. He arrived with this big fanfare. *You know who's coming? Ian Meldrum's coming! Ian Meldrum's coming!* But I thought, *Isn't he the guy who used to mime that 'Winchester Cathedral' song on 'Kommotion'?* He came in, listened to what we were doing and made some momentous comment about me being the next big thing. I remember thinking, *Who is this guy, and why all the fuss?* I'm still wondering.

I don't think 'It's a Man's Man's World' was a very good album – it was pretty cheesy – but it's a landmark in Australian female vocal recordings. It was the first time (with the exception of Wendy Saddington) that an Australian woman really 'tore up the mike', as they say, with completely uninhibited vocals and adventurous, almost masculine phrasing. Members of the session band on that record were Barry Sullivan and Mal Logan, who were both in Chain at the time. Barry ('Big Goose') was one of this country's greatest bass players. He made rhythm-section history with Barry ('Little Goose') Harvey on drums. Together with Phil Manning and Matt Taylor, they also made Aussie-blues history in the early seventies with Chain. Mal played the keyboards with Carson, the 'Canned Heat' of Australia. Broderick Smith was their charismatic lead singer and harmonica player.

Sometime in 1974, Mal joined Chain and he and Barry became the darlings of the Melbourne session scene. They were the young mavericks. They couldn't read a lick of music, but their feel was so good that producers would put in the extra time needed to let them learn their parts. I'm always thankful that Tweed got them on 'It's a Man's Man's World'.

From the getgo I bonded with my two Chain boys. We just immediately hit it off, to the point where during and then after the album was being made, I became one of the family, and their life became my life.

I found a rapport with these two musicians and their friends that I'd never had in Sydney. In Sydney I was a young upstart, but in Melbourne I came to Barry and Mal on an equal level. It was pretty much because of Barry and Mal's friendship that I eventually moved to Melbourne – for their company, their friends and, not least of all, their music. They really cared about me, and seemed to be entertained by my robust personality rather than be annoyed by it. That made me love them all the more. The bond was strong, not just with Barry and Mal but with their friends – Phil Manning, Broderick Smith, Lobby Lloyd – mainly the blues bunch of musicians. It was the lure of that no-nonsense, happy-go-lucky jamming life; so down-to-earth, so real.

I loved the Melbourne music scene, and I loved Melbourne. To me it was, and is, the most fantastic melting pot of a city. With its Greek, Italian and Asian populations, it's like a huge village with an incredible mix of food and cultures. (Let's not forget the coffee.)

Although I was still sort of based in Sydney, I was going back and forth between the two cities. I had a boyfriend in Sydney, but he was married with kids, so I never felt too guilty about being in Melbourne. I stayed at Mal's place, and though it was a mainly happy experience, the only downside was the intense cold in the winter. This was the only thing about Melbourne that was hard to take, especially in those days when the houses young people rented rarely had heating.

My mum at 16, just before the concentration camp.

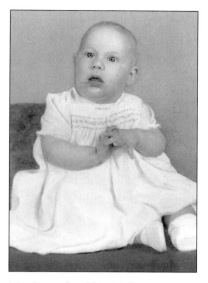

Me, 9 months old in Melbourne — 1953.

Topless on the right with my brothers Robbie (*on left*) and Dennis — 1955.

The Geyer family.

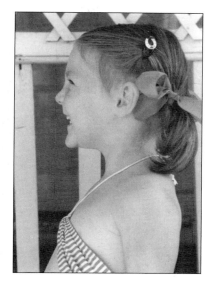

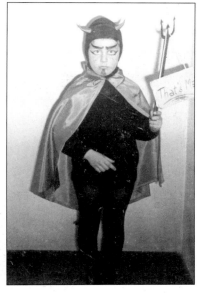

Five years old and 'ready to deal' at a fancy dress party.

Standing on the far left, at Willoughby Girls Primary — 1965.

In the middle, making my fashion
statement at the end-of-year dance at
Willoughby Primary. — 1965.

Aged 16 — 1969.

With Michael Gudinski back stage at the Dallas Brooks Hall in Melbourne — 1976.

A rare, happy moment with Ray Evans — late 1970s.

'Where's One?' From left: Harry Brus, Me, and 'Ted the Head' — 1981.

Sun, my first real band. From left: Me, Keith Shadwick, Gary Norwell, Henry Corey, George Almanza and Chris Sonnenberg — 1972-73.

Mother Earth, From left: Russell Dunlop, Harry Brus, Jim Kelly, Me and Mark Punch — 1973-74.

The *Ready to Deal* Band — 1974-77

Greg Tell — Drums.

Mal Logan — Keyboards.

Mark Punch — Guitar.

Barry Sullivan — Bass Guitar.

The *Ready to Deal* Band on our first *Countdown* — 1975.

In New York at the signing of my Portrait world-record deal for the *So Lucky* album. Paul Schindler and Rob Fraboni (from bottom left). Ray Evans, Lenny Petzie and me (from top right). Others unknown.

It became increasingly harder to go back to Sydney after a spell in Melbourne. I always had such a good time there: the boys were happy to see me and there was always something interesting going on.

It was through Barry and Mal that I met Ray Evans and Michael Gudinski. Chain was managed by Ray at the time, and the band was recording for Mushroom Records, which was co-owned by both Michael and Ray. By the time 'It's a Man's Man's World' came out, it was clear that Ray and Michael were going to become part of my life. I really wanted to be on their label. They started negotiations with RCA to get me over to Mushroom. It was incredibly attractive to me to be with a record company that was like a family, and to be surrounded by people who were genuine music fans. Mushroom was like that then.

In the meantime, Mal, Barry and I started a band called Sanctuary. We got Graeme Morgan on drums, Billy Green on guitar and Keith Sterling on trumpet. People were coming from all over to hear this band.

Billy Green was a very important musician at that time. He had been in Doug Parkinson's In Focus and worked with John McLaughlin's Mahavishnu Orchestra and Weather Report. Billy was one of the musical legends of the seventies. Unbelievably, I hear he no longer plays guitar. He's now playing saxaphone in a covers band somewhere in California.

Graeme Morgan was a big-time session player from years before. He was the elder of the group – a strange, nervy kind of person who dyed his hair jet black. He was the first 'Gothic'-looking guy I'd ever seen. Because of his session work, Graeme couldn't tour with us. We'd leave town and have to hire substitute drummers to sit in with us, like Laurie

Prior, who used to be with Healing Force. Laurie didn't stay for long. We'd do a gig, and the drums would stop or just start banging out of sequence. We'd turn around and he'd be off in the clouds somewhere … Billy Green couldn't always tour with us either. He was off doing his 'Mahavishnu' thing. And Keith Stirling was *always* playing on every session around town that needed horns (no synthesisers in those days). None of these guys really treated Sanctuary as 'their' band, whereas Mal Logan, Barry Sullivan and I really had 'a plan'. Eventually we got John Pugh and Terry Gascgoine on drums, and we toured with that band for a while.

By now, 'It's a Man's Word' had become a bit of a hit. My life was changing, getting busier, and my manager Ray Evans's phone lit up. I'd developed a national profile and Gudinski/Evans were keen to have me start the next album. This was to be my first Mushroom production.

We made the decision to do a band album. We co-wrote and co-produced it together. My dream was to combine my new Melbourne musical family with the ones from Sydney who were the most special. I wanted to play once again with Mark Punch from my Mother Earth days, and I really admired Greg Tell, an incredible black Californian drummer I'd seen at the Whisky-A-Go-Go in Sydney. He'd come out to Australia with a 'doo wop' group for a few seasons and just stayed on. Mark and Greg joined our band and 'Ready to Deal' was born.

We went into Armstrong Studios to write and rehearse the album for about three weeks. Everything, except for 'Heading in the Right Direction' and 'If Loving You is Wrong', was created by the band in that space of time. Mark Punch had written 'Heading in the Right Direction' with Gary Paige a few years earlier, and 'If Loving You is Wrong' was a Luther Ingram song that I'd heard on a Bobby 'Blue' Bland record. We flew Tony Buchanan down from Sydney to play horns and we went to work. With engineer extraordinaire Ernie Rose as co-producer, the whole thing was completed in about seven weeks.

'Ready to Deal', with its mascot single 'Heading in the Right Direction', was the beginning of my real musical career. That was my favourite band. Up until then, no-one in Australia had recorded an original soul record. The way the boys and I played on that record was exactly the way we played live.

Melbourne was becoming the centre of my life and I was becoming a grown-up woman. I even had a live-in boyfriend, and for the first time in my life I became part of 'a couple'.

In those days, anyone who was anyone in rock'n'roll in Melbourne usually went through Mushroom Records or Premier Artists, the agency that Ray and Michael also owned. Both companies were housed in the same building. That place was a conflict-of-interests minefield; there was a string attached to so many acts in Melbourne that came from that building. You had the record company and the booking agency, the management, the people making the posters, everything — all run by the same people, all representing almost every artist in town (and, by now, a lot of the national acts as well). It would never be allowed now, but those were adventurous days and we didn't think that much about it. I guess those who weren't in the 'clique' did think a lot about it ... like, *what about us?* I can relate to that feeling. I've spent some time out of the 'clique' too. Nowadays there's a little more competition, but Premier and its Sydney branch, The Harbour Agency, still pretty much rule the east coast of Australia.

Gudinski's partner at Premier Artists was, and still is, Frank Stivala. He ran the place. If you've ever seen the film *Godfather I*, Frank's like Clemenza. Clemenza was the one who carried out the hits on people, but then he was also the guy who made soup and looked after the Godfather's children when the Godfather got shot. Cooking, stirring, tasting, watching, guarding ... no expression on his huge, Buddha-like face, but powerful. That's Frank, in looks and temperament. In fact, in everything but the hits (although, who knows ...?).

When you go into Premier today there's a main office and then behind a door there's this office with a long desk with guys who all talk like Frank. Kinda like Joe Peschi and Robert DeNiro in *Wise Guys*, except with an Aussie accent. I've always thought someone should write *Premier, The Musical*, and like in the Austen Power's II movie where they have 'Mini Me', there'd be three 'Mini Franks' in the back room. Frank would be singing lines like, 'Dream about it, forget about it!' or 'Take it or leave it!' or 'Look at the fuckin' contract!' In the background there'd be a chorus of Mini Franks singing, 'Yeah yeah, yeah yeah'. And to impress Frank (and they *all* want to impress Frank), the Mini Franks'd yell extra loud while they were shoving it to someone on the phone so Frank would think, 'Ah ... that's my boys!'

Frank and I have always had a pretty good understanding of each other. He's got less ego than anyone I've ever met in this business and, despite the hearsay, he's a straight shooter. (Oops, not that kind of a shooter ... you know what I mean.) He's honest and fair, but I can imagine he'd be formidable if you crossed him.

The girls at Premier are, as they always have been, the real engine room of that place. Whoever the girls are, they always seem to be reincarnated; I've seen about four or five generations come and go. I don't know how they find them – maybe these kinds of girls are drawn to the madness of this kind of job. Some have moved on to become very successful in their own right ('cause when you graduate from the Premier/Mushroom school of hard knocks, you can work anywhere, do anything). These girls have seen and heard it all and nothing shocks them. They have the best sense of humour and they do all the hard work. They can scratch their heads, twirl a tambourine, take a call, type a worksheet and smoke a cigarette ... all while thinking about what they're gonna have for lunch. These are 'can do' girls. They keep the office running on an even keel and rarely moan about it. I love these girls. And they're never paid enough ...

Michael Gudinski is another funny character who still continues to loom large on the music scene. He's a kind of a Clayton's friend in the sense that although we go back a long way, we never really knew each other well. During Mushroom's 25th anniversary celebrations in 1998 I was phoned by a journalist from the *Canberra Times* who was doing a piece on Michael. He said that Michael had told him to call me for some quotes because I was one of his oldest and dearest friends. At first I was flattered, but then I thought, *Wait a minute ... what am I going to say? I don't know him that well.* I don't think too many people know Michael very well. He's a 'meeting-in-a-minute' kind of guy. He seems to run most of his life that way.

We go back twenty-six years, Michael and I, but we've managed to exist only on a parallel plane, never together. I feel close to him by association because of where we come from and what we've been through, but we're not buddies as such.

I've never had a heart-to-heart talk with Michael. It's just never been possible.

Michael is a good business man and always has been, ever since he was a kid running dances in Melbourne. I think he has a knack for sniffing action and then making it work for him. That, and his sheer boyish enthusiasm, are the reasons for his longevity in this business. As a character, he's quite hilarious. With his Krusty-the-Clown hair, his sloping walk and his 'rock'n'roll' soundbites (*'the vibe's good … it's happening'*, *'it's the millennium thing, it's global'*), he's been the object of many a chuckle from artists and colleagues at the functions he presides over (*'and now, without any further ordew …'*).

I think it's sad that Michael hasn't yet conquered the US; it's something he obsesses over and I'm left wondering what my international fate might have been if it hadn't been totally in Michael's hands in the seventies.

In 1984, after nine years with Mushroom, I asked Michael Gudinski if I could get off the label. When the furore of the 'So Lucky' album and 'Say I Love You' died down in the early eighties, that was the beginning of a really difficult music era for me. I was so-called 'over the hill'. There were reviews where they used phrases like 'past her use-by date' … I was thirty.

The music around at the time was not my cup of tea — there was the neo-Romantic craze, as in Duran Duran, Flock of Seagulls, and Australian bands like The Church and INXS. The only black music that was coming out here from America was stuff like Lionel Ritchie, and Michael Jackson's 'Thriller'. They were great pop records but they weren't really R'n'B. In the eighties, Australia didn't have the tolerance for real-roots

R'n'B, and people who played that sort of music were considered 'old blues folk'.

I don't think that Michael, out of loyalty, would have dropped me, but he sure was relieved when I asked to leave. Mushroom was going in a different direction. This was the beginning of the Peter Andre/Kylie Minogue period. He just said OK. So I left Mushroom (I'd already left Ray Evans) and I left Melbourne ... for now.

The last thing I did for Mushroom was 'Trouble in Paradise', a song that Ricky Fataar and I co-wrote and he produced. Ricky was managed by Lydia Livingstone, who also looked after Steven McLean, a very gifted writer and director, and through that connection Steve did the video for the song. I'd first met him years earlier when he was the editor of the music paper *Go-Set*. He interviewed me when I was in Sun. He was a huge Wendy Saddington fan. I remember being so intimidated by him, sitting there at his desk under a huge photograph of Wendy.

I don't remember 'Trouble in Paradise' getting much air time, but it was my favourite video. It was a little black-and-white send-up of French B-grade movies, kind of a 'woman scorned and murders two-timing boyfriend' thing. It had a very prestigious cast – people like Jenny Kee, Martin Sharp, Richard Neville, Penelope Tree. The crew, under Steve McLean's direction, was made up of most of the people from *My Brilliant Career*, who were friends of Steve and Lydia's, and as a favour to them hardly charged us a thing. I found out later that this video made such an impression on certain people, that it was a contributing factor in Steve being given the funding to make a feature movie called *Around the World in Eighty Ways*.

Steve was a big reason I moved back to Sydney. He was an oasis of humour in my dry, dull old rock world. We became really good friends. What I loved about Steve was that he had this amazing cultural knowledge, but a healthy disrespect for same. He was a true bohemian with the humour of Woody Allen and the charm, looks and delicious razor-sharp wit of George Sanders in *All About Eve*. With a rock'n'roll background thrown in for good measure, he was almost a one-man fun park. To this day I think he is one of the funniest people I've ever met.

Steve is a true a fan of great singers. I'm sure he could produce a singer's album if he wanted to. His love of music ranges from the latest Beck recordings to Judy Garland, from Louis Prima to Lou Reed. He's one of those people who cherishes his record collection and plays music as if he needs it to get through his day. He's not someone who puts his CDs on random rotation for background music. He really knows what he wants to hear, and he wants to hear something day and night.

Through Steven McLean I was meeting a lot of people from the arts, not just the music world. Painters, film and theatre people and writers. It wasn't so much what they did that I found attractive as the way they lived their lives. And the humour – in fact, a lot of these folk were nuttier than a fruitcake.

I was asked to do a season at Kinselas in Sydney. Kinselas used to be a famous funeral home, so it's amazing how much frivolity ended up emanating from a place that was steeped in cold, dark exploits at one time (mind you, you could swear the corpses had come back as audience members some nights). Steve directed me in a theatre/cabaret show called 'Soul Cha Cha', which was a sort of autobiographical musical. It was mainly me singing my material, but standing on marks for special lighting. And there was a bit of funny dialogue that Steve wrote. He really thought I was a bit of a comedienne and felt people should see this side of me.

Making this show was one of the happiest periods of my life. But all the rock agents were saying it was career suicide. What was I doing? How could I imagine I could fill six nights a week at Kinselas when hardly anyone would show up at a gig at the Bexley North Hotel? It was a simple theory, really: put me on in a pub where the basic goal of the clientele is to meet up with someone for the night, music being the last thing on their minds, and I'm a dismal failure; but perform in an atmosphere where everything in the club is set up for the show, and add to that the package of dynamic, contemporary music with visual treats and personality, and you can't go wrong.

Word of mouth spread like wildfire through town, and sure enough Kinselas was turning them away by the end. The rock agents were in shock. In the eyes of a lot of rock'n'roll people, doing a dinner show (that's what they called it – a throwback to the RSL days) was considered a sell-out. Nowadays a lot of acts are choosing to perform in these types of venues, but back then it was a brave move.

It was, however, really hard to take one of these shows on the road. The South Australian Arts Council took a later show I'd done at Kinselas on a tour of Adelaide and all these country towns in South Australia. We went down great in Adelaide, but the country was another story. I loved the fact that we were doing outback South Australia and that a lot of Aboriginal people came to see me, some of them travelling from town to town to follow us, but I hated the meanness and the redneck attitude of most of the townspeople. And the venues were generally poor quality. In Port Augusta we were playing in an old school hall in which there was nothing to hang the lights from, literally no fixtures on which to hang the show. Ordinarily, the visual part of the show relied on the way the lighting worked with the music. One half of the show was dark and moody, then there was an interval, and then the other half was bright and full-on. Without the facilities to hang our lights, or use backdrops, or create any sense of mystery, we no longer had the possibility of presenting two different styles, except with the music alone. So, we decided to perform all the music as one show ... one very *long* show. But what we hadn't reckoned on was that the audience had *paid* for an interval. It had been sold as part of the deal, and we had no idea how important this interval was to the audience.

I'd never been in trouble before for not giving ten minutes of *nothing*! Even though it was a marathon of a show, when we came to the end they thought that was the interval and that we would be coming back for another marathon. Somehow, someone forgot to tell the audience that we were presenting it as one show. When they saw us pulling up the equipment and starting to go home, an angry white mob with throbbing red necks chased us back to the motel across the road. I locked myself in my room, terrified, while the throng outside yelled, 'You ripped us off!' We left town real quick. Apparently the next day the headlines of the local paper read: 'RIPPED OFF – GEYER LEAVES AT HALF-TIME!

I guess I can never go back to Port Augusta.

In 1985 there was a book published about Australian rock'n'roll from the early seventies through to the present, compiled by Ed St John for Mushroom Records. Everyone who even made a burp on a record was in there, but they completely left me out. There was not even a mention of my name. It was as if I'd never existed! I was in shock.

I ran into Ed St John somewhere and asked him why I wasn't in that book. He said it was probably because I didn't have any records out at the time. Also, he thought that I was getting out of the rock'n'roll business and moving into 'cabaret'. *Huh …?* And Mushroom, what about Mushroom? Michael later told me that he didn't know I wasn't in it. He hadn't even looked at it.

I was amazed that my whole past had been erased. I don't think it was malicious; that's the sad part. They just plain forgot about me. Seems like a small thing now, but at the time it hit me like a bullet.

I tried to carry on through the eighties after Mushroom let me go. I approached Warner Brothers (WEA) – just rang up without representation, made an appointment and went by myself to talk to Peter Ikin, head of A&R at the time. My spiel must have been good because he signed me immediately. 'Sing to Me' was the album that resulted, and I have to say it was a stinker. It was probably the single most terrible record I've ever made. There were no redeeming features (well, maybe just the title track, a Don Walker song). I was a music moron.

After one single, Warners dropped me, and Peter Ikin sent my representative at the time a letter. It said something like, 'We really respect Renée as one of our great singers but we don't think that her greatness as a singer translates to record sales.' In other words, you're OK, but get out of the recording business. It's like they were saying, give up. First of all I was hurt and lay in bed and moped around the house for four days, feeling sorry for myself, but then vanity got the better of me. It was time to get on with it.

I made plans to get out of Australia. I sold my furniture and my car and stored all my beloved 'chatchkas' at my mother's house. After a couple of weeks' worth of shows, with $10 000 in my pocket, I was off to New York in a puff of smoke.

That was the beginning of my nine-year stay in America.

Chapter 5

MUSICIANS

I've learned almost everything I know about music from musicians. I realised very young that I needed the best to make me be the best. I knew I needed them real bad.

At a time when most young women my age were out socialising, I was on the road with an all-boy band. These were my companions.

In my life I have worked with all types of musicians. There are many hybrids and combinations of personalities, but generally, within the five categories I'm about to describe, you pretty much have the characteristics that made up a band in the seventies.

First there's the one I call Nut Man. He's the fastidious musician, usually pristine in appearance and in the playing of his instrument. Very anal. This is the guy who was into computer equipment before its dawn. Nut Man doesn't drink very much, but when he does he gets drunk after one drink. He's says he's a vegetarian, though when the food is free, he's in there, usually digging into the meat goods. He eats nuts – lots of them. Hence his name. Always a soiled brown paper bag full of nuts. Maybe a little cheese too. And some dried fruit ... You can always tell where this guy is by the trail of nut shells he leaves behind. He's usually unhappy about anyone smoking or drinking around him, and he always speaks in lowered tones. You've got to lean in very close to hear him talk, and when you do you realise he's not saying much. When the others get up to their hijinx, Nut Man is always watching with his bag of nuts. *Salt free*. He is the only one who isn't born a gifted musician. He's planned it; and he's studied it.

Very rarely has a Nut Man lasted very long in one of my bands.

Next is Open Man. I call him that because he's like an open wound. Emotionally and physically he's open to everything. He's usually sloppy, sweet, warm, loving, naughty, and smelly. Open Man is also an op-shop man. I reckon he'd even buy second-hand underpants if he could – anything for a bargain, he's there. He is extremely well-hung. This man is the main getter of sexual action in the group, but it's always on his own – never as part of a dare or a group thing. *This guy is serious*. He needs his action and he goes out and gets it. He disappears, and you always know what he's up to. He's the type who *seriously* thinks he's doing a girl a favour and giving her life some beauty and education by sleeping with her.

And it has to be said, he's an extraordinary naturally-gifted musician.

Now we come to Book Man. There's always one person in the band who's really smart academically – the private-school-boy type who really hates the music business but *has* to be in it because he was born to it. Everything is sort of beneath him, and in the clear light of day he thinks that everything about being in the music industry is ridiculous – and he moans about it at length. *It all is*, of course, but when you're on the road you just don't want to keep hearing about it, day in day out.

Book Man plays music from his heart, but he doesn't understand the beast within. He has the soul of a street minstrel but was brought up in a sheltered and privileged environment, so he's torn; he loves and curses his talent at the same time. Everything he really hates and looks down upon is really *him*. He'll look at a cover of a great sixties black album and mock the pimpish nature of the clothes, or the sheer brazenness of someone's pose, and yet these are his favourite records. When he's not playing his instrument, Book Man is a clean, white, snobby, pasty man with just a hint of a baby-vomit smell about him. He's incredibly gifted and, like Open Man, a natural soul man.

Open Man loves Book Man. (Open Man loves everybody.) Book Man hates Open Man, but *loves* his playing.

Then you have Mean Man. This is generally your alcoholic musician, usually a horn player, who thinks everyone is inferior to himself. He ridicules mankind in general for what he considers to be their faults, yet *he* has more of them than anyone. He has many deep-seated problems, I think – possibly as a result of an abusive childhood. But he hasn't, and probably won't, come out of the closet about it. For all this, he plays brilliantly, if inconsistently. Like most extraordinary players, whichever way you want to look at it his talent is either a gift or an affliction given to him at birth.

Mean Man can be very funny, and he's super-intelligent too, but he has a mean streak. He wants to be like the academic Book Man – he lives in the places Book Man grew up, and is probably married to a Book Woman – but Mean Man comes from the wrong side of the tracks. He becomes very nasty when he drinks, his meanness taking over the sweet part of his personality. If fans should come backstage to see me and I'm not there, Mean Man will greet them with verbal torture, because he knows they're not there to see *him*.

Now, Boo-Boo Man. This is the guy who's partial to the odd mind-altering substance. I call him Boo-Boo Man because, ever since I can remember, whenever I had any illegal substance I called it 'boo-boo'. When you're little, a boo-boo is a mistake … a sweet mistake. I *love* Boo-Boo Man. He has the most easy-going, beautiful temperament of all the guys. You feel like you're with the coolest crowd when you hang out with him and his friends. He's very handsome, and he's always smoking. At night-time, when the cigarettes are alight, the smell is delicious; in the day, not so delicious. But it's always a joy to hang out with Boo-Boo Man. He and I might separate from the rest of the band after a show, usually with a member of the road crew who is also happy to indulge, and get up to mischief together. *Hey*, it's better than eating health foods with Nut Man, or drinking a bottle of bourbon with Mean Man, or discussing what a horrible mess we are in with Book Man, and it certainly beats following Open Man around in his pursuit of the fresh catch of the day. Nuts, booze, philosophy and getting girls? *No thanks!* Drugs? *OK …*

Remember, I wasn't just out with inane junkies. These were my compadres, my buddies. I loved and respected these guys. I felt safe. We just had this *little* flaw ... we used to live for our little reward after performing our rock'n'roll duties for the night.

Now that you've met the types of guys I used to live and work with, let me try to take you through a typical day in the life of this band on tour.

I don't do many country towns these days, not since I've been managing myself. I only go if the money's good or if somebody really wants me there. But at one time country towns were my bread and butter, and it's the memories of those tours that really sum up what it's like to be in a band, especially in the seventies.

So, we're on the road, travelling from one small country town to another ...

The day starts when you're woken up wherever you're staying. It takes about an hour for everyone to get it together. Boo-Boo Man and I are usually the first ones ready. In country towns there's no action, chemically or in any other way, so for once we get a good night's sleep and we're up-and-at-'em pretty early. Nut Man is a little late because he's at the health food shop getting more nuts for the day ahead. Mean Man and Book Man are both incredibly hung-over, running late and very repentant. They both did and said some really bad things the night before, and are like quiet little mice for the first few hours of the trip. Open Man is last, because he's in the other people's rooms scavenging. If you left behind a piece of bread, some salami or a half-drunk bottle of orange juice, Open Man will grab it and put it in his case for later. 'You never know,' he'll say.

As we motor on from one town to the next we hear from Open Man how he made some country-town girl's life more meaningful last night, and I'm thinking to myself, *I hope she's got antibiotics!* Open Man doesn't like to shower, because he wants to savour the aroma from the night before. This, together with the smell of two-day-old salami sandwiches, stale beer from the night before and old chocolate milk, makes for a most unusual aroma in the vehicle. Oh, and Boo-Boo Man's cigarettes ... Gotta have cigarettes.

So we're all in the van/car/bus – whatever we have at the time – and I'm in the front next to the driver. I've always had a fear of the driver falling asleep at the wheel, but there's more chance of him dying from me talking him to death than there is from him falling asleep on the road. Racing to get to the next gig, it's easy to have accidents on the road. We never did. Touch wood, we've been really lucky.

There are always too many people who smoke (everyone but Nut Man). It's a travelling cloud. The vehicle flies along with smoke pouring out from each window. It's like a car on fire, but with no flames.

And we drive and drive and drive ... I hate it. I'm a hopeless passenger; I'm always impatient to get there.

Are we there yet?

The first stop is for bacon and eggs. I am always the instigator of stopping at a diner. Everyone else is 'No, no, no', but of course when we do stop they're all into it. The smoking vehicle pulls up and out we jump, as if riding into Dodge City, with the saloon doors swinging. *Bacon and eggs. And make it snappy!* There is always someone in the band who gives the impression of the outlaw as we walk through the door. There's always that 'us and them' mentality. The road-stop people eye us with suspicion.

I worship the shrine of the egg and don't think of it as just a cake ingredient. So I was always upset by the state of the eggs at those diners. If you asked for a poached or fried egg you got something like a golf ball, so rather than explaining that you wanted it less hard you would just say, *Scramble 'em. Cook the suckers to within an inch of their googy-egg life.* That way they couldn't go wrong. The bacon was always chewy, never crispy, and there was always water at the bottom of the plate. I always wondered where that water came from. This was followed by a weak cup of tea. And so, that was breakfast.

Open Man never orders anything – he knows there'll be some fine pickin's for him at the end of everyone else's meal. Book Man and Mean Man usually stay in the car during the breakfast stop, still hung-over. Boo-Boo Man gets more cigarettes. Nut Man orders a lovely plate of lettuce and tomato but enviously eyes off everyone else's plates.

Any further stops are made more out of boredom than hunger – usually to get more cigarettes. Or we stock up on lollies and cakes and eat ourselves into some sick oblivion until the next town. Wait … something's wrong … we need more smoke. Oh yes, here come the joints.

Are we there yet?

In the car, in the front seat, I'm thinking, *What will I do when I get to town? Maybe I'll go to Woolworths.* I could somehow always spend fifty bucks or more just on 'stuff' – anything from make-up to hair accessories to floaties for the hotel swimming pool. *Hey, maybe I'll go to a saddlery shop and buy some stirrups? I really need some stirrups. Maybe some spurs. Yeah ... And maybe some ugh boots. The possibilities are mindless – I mean endless!*

Such is the lot of a city-born person travelling in the country. There's never much to do in these towns unless they're on the coast and it's summer. The beach makes up for a lot of things. My bands always loved touring in summer.

Are we there yet?

After an eternally long drive the smokemobile arrives in the town we're working that night. After Woolies, I go straight to my room at the motel and make sure there's a TV and a phone. (In some of these towns in the seventies that was a tall order, but for me the TV and the telephone were a must. They took away the loneliness. I didn't necessarily watch the TV, but it had to be on. To this day I'm addicted to the TV and the telephone.)

In my room I switch on the TV, pull the blankets off the bed and toss them back on so they're not so tucked in, throw some sarongs over the couches for colour and light some incense. Now the room is mine and it's nap time.

Meanwhile, the band scouts the town. Boo-Boo Man might check to see if there are any goodies for later. Open Man sniffs around for a girl. Mean Man makes sure the backstage drink rider is there. Book Man sulks in his room. And Nut Man, well, you know what Nut Man is doing ... *Salt free.*

From about four o'clock on, everyone starts revving up. That's when the soundcheck usually is and it's when we all remember why we're here. By the time the gig comes we *really* know why we're here. Everybody looks at each other. *Wow! You've come up pretty good!* During the day no-one has looked each other in the eye, for one reason or another. But at show time everyone brushes up so well. This is what we were born to do; this is our shining hour.

The dressing rooms were pretty bad. Some places still had a convict mentality towards musicians and their place in the world. Rock music was never considered 'a show'. *Why would musos want dressing rooms? They're just playing music.* To this day I can put lipstick on without a mirror, and do it faster than a speeding bullet. Without a smudge I can perfectly outline the form of my lips, fill them in, gloss them, do the whole thing. People say, 'How did you do that?' *Practice.* No mirrors for twenty years.

The gig is the exciting bit. You get up and do the show and you are satisfied. Because even if the audience isn't one with the band, the band is one with the band, and that is what's important. All the angst from the day – everything – is forgotten for those one or two hours. All that's left is the sheer respect and awe that these people – Open Man, Nut Man, Book Man, Mean Man and Boo-Boo Man – have for each other. No-one in their right mind would live a life like this unless there was a reason. *This* is the reason.

After the show, no-one comes backstage for at least fifteen or twenty minutes until we cool down. Mainly me and the drummer, that is. He is the only other truly physical member of the band. We're usually in the band room alone, sitting there panting. When you've been yelling for two hours, which is basically what I do, you just want to veg out. The sound of your voice has been paramount in your head for two hours so you just want to sit there and be very quiet.

It's a strange way to live. After a sedentary existence all day, sitting in a car full of smoke, eating rubbish and not being good to your body, you then become a physical and emotional athlete for this one- or two-hour period at night. Every day is the pursuit of getting to the next place for that emotional display. From the waist up, it really is athletes' stuff.

The only person who comes off stage without a streak of sweat or nary a flush in his cheeks is Nut Man, because he's a made musician – he has studied, and he's well-equipped. His emotions have nothing to do with his playing. (These guys last forever in the business.) He is always resented at the end of the gig, because he's there looking at us poor sweating schmos and thinking, *These guys wouldn't sweat so much if they just stopped eating meat.*

If the boys got any of the songs wrong during the show I'd confront them immediately after in the band room, because even though I was drained there was always just enough breath left to point out the mistakes of the night. I'm not the most diplomatic person, not good at holding it in. But my criticisms are usually very quick and fairly painless. I liked to deal with it straight away, and then it's over.

Once the crowd starts leaving and the tour manager's picked up the money, I get escorted back to the hotel. It's very hard to go to sleep after a gig – you have to let off steam for at least a couple of hours. When the drained feeling wears off, you're exhilarated. It's like throwing water on a fire: for a minute the heat's gone, but then the embers come back. You haven't put out the fire.

That's when the self-destructive streak sometimes comes into play, when you're in some little town where there's really no place to go and you're left to your own devices. That's where a musician's bad habits start. Here comes the sexual need, the chemical need, the alcoholic need, or just the verbal-abuse need. Nowadays people have learned to cope.

They might do yoga, they might have herbal aids. There's all sorts of things people have learned to do in the last twenty years to cope with these sorts of feelings and to channel them properly so that they're not in a bad mental place. It's become a New Age industry. But in those days it was the Wild West.

In the big cities, after the show you'd go out to some club and hear another band play, but in these country towns, what are you gonna do? Anyone with half an artistic bone in their body who lives in these places has usually got the hell out of there. *Why wouldn't they?* There's no action in these towns in any shape or form. *We* bring the action.

With nothing to do, and just the drink rider at our disposal, everyone goes back to one of the guys' rooms and tries to drum up a bit of a party. There's always something going on. Someone might put a porno flick in the video machine and, with the sound turned off, I provide the voice of the tortured female or the torturer. Someone else might do commentary like Ritchie Benaud for the cricket, describing what's happening with what orifice and what implement. Mindless, but hilarious.

We sit around and have discussions about all the other musicians and bands. Someone will have a tape of some great American musician, which makes it easier to rip apart local musos. There'll always be some critical but very funny remark about somebody who I'm sure is sitting in some other motel room in some other country town, saying the same things about us. After we've dissected every local musician we can think of, and had the usual philosophical argument about *what's more important? – technique or feel?* (this one's a must for late-night discussions . . . no-one ever wins in this debate), I bid my goodnights and leave the boys still smoking, drinking and generally screaming with laughter at each other. I'm usually next door. Somehow I'm always put next door to the loudest guy. I can hear them all through the night.

And as I drift off to sleep in my room, Open Man is returning to the room next door to talk about the woman he had last time in this town but couldn't find tonight. Nut Man will be tucked in bed with his nuts and fruit under his pillow. Book Man will be telling Open Man he's a piece of shit, that he's no good for this world. Mean Man is having another drink and telling Book Man to shut up and leave Open Man alone, and that he's really not as academic as he thinks he is anyway. Boo-Boo Man will be in the corner, pissed off that he has to listen to this rubbish. (Eventually he'll shuffle off to his room, take a couple of Mersyndols and drift off … better than nothing.)

As I lie there listening to this madness, hoping Mean Man and Book Man don't come to fisticuffs so I have to fly new musicians in the next day, I think to myself that I am a part of all of these people. I am a musician, whatever that means. In a way, I'm a bit like Book Man in that I am the thing I can't stand.

But when you look at my life, they *are* my life. Most things I've learned, I've learned from them, with them, through them or in spite of them. I am all those people all wrapped up in one.

Except Nut Man.

Chapter 6

MISMANAGING THE UNMANAGEABLE

My voice has been the source of all my money and of my carelessness with money.

I've earned so much in my career, yet I have little to show for it.

I have a sort of healthy disrespect for it, which is why it's been so easy to come by, and in turn so elusive. I've always thought, *Ah, there's more where that came from ... Just book another show, it'll be OK.* The money I've made has gone mainly on knick-knacks, meaningless 'chatchkas' that in retrospect seem so silly but at the time of purchase, pure bliss. A little jewellery here, a little make-up there, a couch thrown in for good measure, clothes, crockery, cutlery, bathmats, an ottoman or two, vintage teapots, paintings ... You get the picture. There's no rhyme or reason ... just stuff.

Oh, and magazines, lots and lots of magazines. To this day, I love consuming trash literature. When I lived in the United States it was like living in a media Disneyland. I could be down to my last thin dime and then, when I finally got some precious cash, I'd buy $100 worth of mags instead of putting food into the cupboard. I did that many times – *Vanity Fair*, *Harper's Bazaar*, *The Face*, *Star*, *National Enquirer*, all the daily newspapers, *Rolling Stone*, French *Vogue*, Italian *Vogue*, American *Vogue* ...Vogue schmogue Vogue*@%#!

The first job I got was as a typing clerk at the Law Society of New South Wales, for $29 a week. This was 1970 and that was the average wage for my age, but I immediately had bigger fish to fry and so befriended the switchboard operator to get some lessons at lunchtime. This was no mean feat ... we're talking the 'Sylvester', the mother of all switchboards. If you could operate this baby, you could get a job anywhere. You might remember Lily Tomlin's character Ernestine, the one who snorted when she laughed. *She* used a Sylvester. Somehow, I don't think she would have been as funny using some streamlined two-line intercom. I loved it: all those plugs connecting into all those holes (and the odd eavesdrop didn't go astray either).

My second and last steady job was at the Country Party head office. I got the job as receptionist by lying about my age and my qualifications in general. I'd only been at the last job for six months, but I had no time to dilly-dally: if I was going to start buying chatchkas I'd better start earning some decent money. My music hadn't sustained me financially yet, and I needed *stuff*!

They offered me $45 a week. *When do I start?* I lasted there maybe three months. I liked the people I worked with. In fact, they were very understanding and patient with me, considering my tardiness most mornings and general lack of interest in the proceedings ... *Good morning, may I help you? One moment, please.* I must admit that I loved the theatre of the 'phone greeting' in the beginning. The novelty wore off real quick, though.

After the Country Party I joined an agency that booked temporary office work. No sooner had I started than I was moving swiftly down the ladder of officedom. They would call me up at random to fill in for some sick secretary or receptionist. Sometimes I was up for it, sometimes I wasn't ... especially when there was no Sylvester to play with. I always made friends with the older girls at these jobs and had some fun going out with them from time to time, but in the end the jobs bored the shit out of me and the agency eventually gave up on me. It didn't matter anyway, because by now I was really starting to get *gigs*.

My first manager was Horst Leopold. He originally managed the band Sun, and when I left them and joined Mother Earth, he came too. He was nice enough, aside from the fact that through him I ended up almost signing my life away to RCA. There was apparently no exit clause in that contract, and I'd probably still be stuck in some kind of RCA/BMG limbo if Michael Gudinski and Ray Evans hadn't come along.

I first met Ray when I came to Melbourne to record 'It's a Man's Man's World'. Barry Sullivan and Mal Logan from Chain played on that record, and Ray was managing them at the time. Horst had by then moved to New York, so Ray took over my management.

RCA weren't terribly committed to a worldwide career for me and told me they didn't think I was ready. *Not ready? I was born ready!* Again, I had bigger fish to fry. Michael and Ray apparently thought so too and so went about the task of getting me out of my never-ending deal with RCA. It was a big job, but it ended up that Mushroom promoted 'Man's World' and the single 'Sunday Morning', and an agreement was made that Mushroom would produce the next few albums but that RCA would distribute them.

This was 1974. I was oblivious to all the red-tape goings on. All I knew was that I was thrilled to be a Mushroom artist – even though, as part of the deal, my records were still to carry an RCA label for another seven years.

I loved my life in Melbourne at this time. I enjoyed the fact that my manager was co-owner of my record company as well as the touring agency, Premier/Harbour, which handled the biggest acts at the time. Such conflict of interest may well have been frowned upon in some other parts of the Western world, but here in the wild early days of Oz rock ... anything went. Anyway, I was the Golden Girl there for a while and was looked after pretty well. I never wanted for anything (except a bank account). More about that later ...

I'd been staying at Mal Logan's house in Malvern around this time. Ray and Michael lived in a big two-storey house on Toorak Road. There was a swimming pool in the front garden and lots of space, so when they offered me a room, it made sense to move in.

Most people who came to the house hung out in the living area to the left of the entrance, but if there were lots of people around they would spill into the right one too. When you walked into the house, the staircase was right in front of you and led up to a kind of mezzanine where the bedrooms were. Mine was on the left, Michael's on the right, a spare room was directly ahead, and the huge one at the front belonged to Ray. When I drive past that house now it's like when you're little and you think where you lived was so huge, but actually it's not. It's just a large Tudor-type house, by no means the mansion I always thought it was.

We all had our separate lives. I was totally into my band, Ray was collecting cars, and Michael was the devoted record-company man. He spent morning, noon and night at the office. The three of us would only come together if there was some party at the house, or if we'd pass each other in the hall in the morning or at the end of the day. The fun times, the notorious times, were few and far between, although they of course are the times people like to reminisce about the most. There were Skyhooks parties, Split Enz parties. Whoever the major artist was at the time, there'd be a party for them. I'd often come home from doing a show to find my manager and the head of Mushroom records entertaining some girls they'd met at a gig. There'd be the remains of a party up the stairs – a bra here, pantyhose there, scrambled eggs on the walls … Michael and I had a few romantic liaisons in that house – nothing too deep (if you knew Michael as I did back in those days … nothing was ever too deep). But, far from public perception, there were never these 'threesomes' people have wondered about. We were just a Jewish girl, a Jewish boy and an accountant.

The people who came to that house were mostly friends of Michael and Ray's. Michael had parties, mainly for fun and letting off steam because he worked so hard. Ray, however, was more into the 'business-enhancing' kind of party. I guess today you'd call it networking. Although between us was non-existent communication, he was a good networker. I eventually moved out of that house, soon after 'Ready to Deal' was released.

I never had much in common with Ray, and yet he handled everything to do with my business life and made all my career decisions. There weren't many discussions about what or where I'd perform, just a phone call to let me know what would be happening and what time I had to be there. I didn't like him. He was unfeeling and dismissive – not someone you could take your troubles to and confide in. I figured, well he's no Mother Teresa, but at least he seems to be good at his job … and I was working.

I must have seemed like a bit of a bitch in those days, because whenever I was around Ray in public I was always in a bad mood. I felt like an employee doing a job. I never got to see the fruits of my hard work doing press interviews and the like, so I was always a little disgruntled. Back then I never experienced the thrill of the strategy and then the 'pay-off'. Alot of the time there *was* no strategy. (Lots of pant-seats flying, but no strategy.) If I did a show and it was a sell-out, I never knew the joy of receiving a cheque. Every now and then, Ray and Michael would high-five each other after a show and I'd be with the band on the other side of the band room wondering what all the fuss was about …

Money, that's what it was all about. I have to be honest, I was never really driven by the money part of success. I never insisted that Ray show me receipts or invoices … I just thought it would all be OK and life seemed to be good.

In 1974, the Liberal Party approached Ray to ask me to sing their campaign song for the Federal election that year.

It was called 'Turn on the Lights'. Now this was the election just before the Whitlam dismissal. Things were hotting up politically and Labor had only just scraped in. It was an emotionally charged time for those who followed politics. I had no idea what I was walking into – politics was the furthest thing from my mind in those days. They offered us $1000 for me to sing the song – a fortune at that time. There was no discussion with Ray as to whether this was a good career move or not. I had no idea of what the repercussions of a decision like this might be ... but I found out the hard way.

On the tour I did following that election, I found that my crowds had dwindled, especially in Canberra, Melbourne and Adelaide. People were disappointed that I had contributed to the election of a government that at that time a lot of people thought was immoral and incompetent. I still get the odd negative comment about my involvement even now. I've become a little better informed than I was in those days and I would never do it if I had my time again. I'd love to think that all kinds of people would find something attractive about my music, regardless of their political persuasion.

In 1978, Ray brought the Supremes out to tour Australia (Mary Wilson was the only original one left). Mary's husband, and the manager of the group, was Pedro Ferrer, a handsome, dashing black Puerto Rican. Very smooth, a real operator. Unbeknownst to me, Ray, having lost on the tour and owing Pedro money, made a bit of a deal with him: on my next trip to America, Pedro was to represent me. Apparently he'd heard one of my records, thought there was some future in my working in the United States and, instead of Ray paying him back his money, had negotiated to take over my management in the America.

All this was done without my knowledge, of course. Ray just intimated to me that Pedro was helping him out over there, and wasn't it great to have such a wonderful guy working with us? I thought so too, for a minute. After all, Pedro was also managing Marvin Gaye at the time ... *Wow, I might get to meet him!* Nope, never did. I found out later that this was Marvin's bankrupt period and it was not long before his daddy shot him dead on his birthday.

I did find it odd that Ray was never around when Pedro was. What I didn't realise was that he'd literally handed me over like a piece of meat ... sold my soul to a Puerto Rican devil!

Pedro seduced me a couple of times. I have to admit that for a while there I was very willing; he was devastatingly attractive and I was completely under his spell. But the novelty of Pedro started wearing thin when he began sending over these parking-attendant-type thugs, who couldn't speak English, to bring me my allowance for the month. I was living with some Aussie girls in an apartment at the time and these boys wanted to 'party'! They'd say (through the chain-bolted door, 'cause they were *not* coming in), 'Hey, Pedro say it OK we come over, OK?' It was definitely *not* OK!

I never had any work during this period – no sessions, no gigs, just my allowance and Pedro telling me how it was gonna be. He was incredibly controlling in a hypnotic kind of way, and when I finally snapped out of my stupor I'd argue with him. He eventually learned that I was not mouldable and that there was no future with me, business-wise. I'm sure he was as happy to see me go as I was to leave him; it was very much a mutual thing. I've seen him recently and we've had a chuckle about those days. He's still devastatingly handsome.

Meanwhile, *where was Ray?* I suppose I'm kind of slow to learn sometimes. In retrospect it appeared to me that Ray had palmed me off without a thought of what would happen to me. I've never forgotten that one . . . that one's real hard to forgive.

I liked Ray's wife Judith very much. She was a beautiful English girl who had somewhat of a calming influence on proceedings. When she and Ray asked me and Michael Gudinski to be godparents to their son Jason, we agreed. I don't think we were worthy of the honour and I've always felt bad about taking on such an important role as flippantly as I did. We never really kept in touch through Jason's life and only recently did I run into him at a 'Vibes on a Summer's Day' dance fest that I was performing at. He's a beautiful, charming young man and I'm proud to be his godmum. Ray and Judith split up years ago and she has virtually brought him up alone – and magnificently.

As time went on, I found myself increasingly resentful of Ray. I noticed his lifestyle seemed to become more extravagant while mine was deteriorating *and* I was still working non-stop. I couldn't understand it. When he bought a beautiful heritage home in Brighton while I was struggling to rent somewhere much humbler, I didn't feel right about it. You see, with Ray, I had my rent paid, got shoes and clothes if I needed them (after an argument or three) and got pocket money here and there, but I never actually received a royalty statement, and I never had money put into an account. (I never *had* an account.) I didn't even know how to write a cheque. There was never a statement or even a general chat about my finances.

When I came back to Melbourne in the early eighties, I rented an apartment in Middle Park. I had no furniture or household goods. I was coming back after living in the US doing the 'So Lucky' sessions. There was a resurgence in my popularity when 'Say I Love You', the single, came out. It was a big hit in Australia and things must have been good because Ray let me have $5000 to set up house. It hit home a little later that I must have been worth a *lot* more than $5000 with 'So Lucky' becoming my biggest-selling album ever. But I still had to beg for that five. I don't think Ray intended to rip me off or stop me from getting my dues. I just think he was arrogantly careless a lot of the time.

By the late seventies Ray managed other people like Molly Meldrum, Derryn Hinch, and Russell Morris ... All of these artists, by the way, have also left Ray.

I stuck with Ray for all those years because it was too hard to get out. It was too much trouble and I was working all the time ... In my stomach I felt that it was going to come to a head one day, but I would ignore my gut feeling till a few years later.

Finally, in about 1983, when things weren't so great and record sales had dropped, I was like a wombat, walking blindly until it finally hits the wall and looks up and says, oh! I was living in the spare room of a friend's house and Ray was in his mansion in Brighton. Where was my money? According to Ray, there was none. It had all been spent. *On what? OK ...* There was no record of where it had all gone, no statements of royalties, no tour income or expense records. Nothing for me to look at so as to understand why there was no money after nine years of hard work.

I got the hell out of Melbourne to get some objective space between me and the mess, and hired a lawyer to advise me on how to leave Ray. At this point, I didn't even want money, I just wanted *out*. That was the beginning of the end of Ray Evans and me. The lawyer, Phil Dwyer, immediately wrote a letter to him initiating the split. We were all shocked when Ray wrote back to him saying, yes, that would be fine, as soon as I paid the $70000-odd that was owed by my touring company, which he was overseer of.

I found out that there was indeed a lot of money owed to a multitude of creditors, mostly really hard-working small businesses, like the people who put up posters, the truck companies, the equipment hirers. Some of the bills were as small as $60. There were big ones too, but most were for the little businesses who'd helped me get on the road. Some of the bills were years old. It was pathetic ... and all in my name.

I think Phil Dwyer would have loved to have taken that boy to court to fight it and audit him for the last nine years, but I insisted that I just wanted to move on and never lay eyes on Ray Evans again. I've never seen a lawyer so fired up and ready to pounce like Phil was. He was truly disgusted. Ray Evans doesn't know how lucky he was.

Anyway, through Phil we hired the accountant John Smith and we went about the task of bringing the amount down by scrutinising those bills. I ended up with a bill of $45000 to settle. These were the accounts with my name actually on them. The rest was Ray's problem. *I was free!*

For the first time in my life, I called and spoke to all the creditors. I explained that I was leaving my manager and taking matters into my own hands with the help of my lawyer and accountant, that I wanted to pay back every cent that was owed and could I make some sort of monthly payment plan? All of them, without exception, were thrilled to get the call, and especially happy that I was no longer with Ray Evans. They all believed me when I told them I had no knowledge that they had been owed this money for so long. Every creditor made it so easy for me to make my payments, and I did. I just paid them all off, bit by bit.

I was starting on a new adventure, and though I was a little scared at first, the joy of doing different kinds of venues and actually getting paid at the end of the night soon took care of that. I started singing at places like the Basement in Sydney, and its equivalent (or as near as could be found) in other cities. I also did more theatrical shows like Kinselas in Sydney. My creative juices were flowing in my musical life and in my business life too. I was choosing the kinds of places I'd work, and I only worked when I wanted to work. Not only was I doing venues where people actually came specifically to hear me sing, but I was negotiating my fees to boot! I remember, when I first started doing the Basement, that hordes of people would be lining up to get in. It was dizzying. There I was on stage, pretending to be enthralled by the guitar solo, and actually counting heads! I've calmed down a bit since then but I still get a big thrill at the sight of a full house.

At times it can get a bit much managing yourself, but I think I've got the hang of it now. I have a lot of help. Frank Stivala at Premier Artists in Melbourne is still my agent, except this time there's no middleman. He and the girls in that office are gems. They are very understanding and patient with me.

I've often thought that I might like to find another manager to help me with my career, but really, there isn't anyone in this country who can do for me what I can't already do for myself. I guess I'm a bit skittish about even the word 'manager' now, let alone entrusting my career to someone again. Still, as I said, I have a wonderful agent, a trustworthy accountant who sends me statements *monthly*, and good old Phil Dwyer, who still handles my legal business.

I'm a bit of a handful (Paul Kelly didn't write the song 'Difficult Woman' for me for nothin'), so I am in awe of these people's loyalty to me when the going gets tough. But I hope I'm honourable in some kind of way, and worth the trouble.

I still struggle a little with money, every now and then. You see, I can't seem to give up buying *stuff*. I'm definitely improving, though.

Anyone know of a Chatchkas Anonymous anywhere?

Chapter 7

DRUGS

I've died three times.

Overdosed ... heart stopped beating ... blue in the face for twenty minutes ... had to be revived. That kind of died.

When you're on heroin and you OD, you don't remember anything. You're just out. But apparently your breathing stops, your heart stops, and you have to be kept awake so things don't stop long enough for your entire body to stop. What happens when the paramedics finally come, is that they give you a shot of Narcan, which is an antidote for any kind of opiate. But before people like that can arrive there's the 'last resort' rescue mission, which means the people you did it with smacking and pinching you and trying to keep you alive. You feel euphoric when you wake up. You're loaded.

The first time I overdosed was in a friend's house in Elsternwick in Melbourne in the mid-seventies. That time they didn't call the paramedics, but they were about to, because I was gone for about twenty minutes. Blue. Dead.

I always had someone administer heroin. I could never do it myself (it's amazing how willing I was to have a needle and yet, in a normal medical situation, needles frightened the hell out of me). Present at this sordid event were three friends: a well-known singer from a band of the time, a drummer, and one of the musicians in my band. We used to meet up after our gigs and partake. They were my gang.

It was a very reckless procedure and almost always, in those days, someone would have too much, mainly because of the uncertainty of how strong the stuff was. There were no labels or instructions on how to safely administer heroin. This particular time it was me who took too much.

Back in those days I was already quite famous, and these people were panicking, wondering what they should do. If I died they'd have lost a friend, sure, but that was the last thing on their minds. Foremost was the fact that this was *big trouble*.

Should they split? The singer did ... I would have too. There were enough people taking care of me. The repercussions would have been huge. Besides, the fun definitely goes out of the evening when someone ODs.

I woke up and these two guys were hitting me. *Why are you hitting me?* To keep me awake they were also talking at me and dragging me along the gravel road outside. I was wearing black tights and they completely wore through. I still have scars on all my toes from that night.

The next day I was to appear on 'Countdown'. I had to wear platform shoes with a strap that went across my poor

My uncle Borach at the Old South Head
Synagogue in Sydney

Winner...? What was I thinking?

With Mal Logan on stage in
Melbourne — 1976.

At Mushroom's 10th Anniversary at
Myer Music Bowl in Melbourne.

At a Mushroom party with Michael Hutchence and Greg McCainsh — 1983.

With Penelope Tree whilst making 'Trouble in Paradise' video — 1984.

The making of 'Trouble in Paradise' video — 1984.

At a fundraiser for one of Princess Anne's charities in London. From left: Pamela Stephenson, John Farnham and me — 1985.

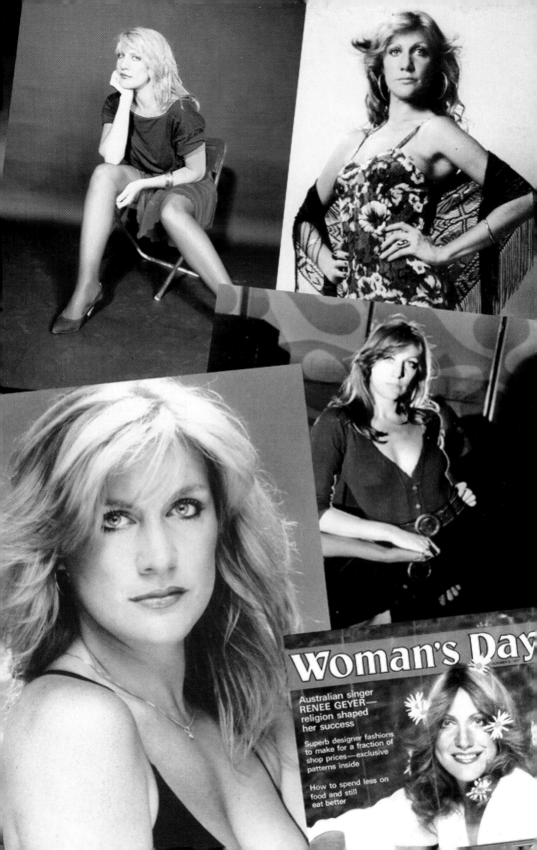

Some of my favourite musical characters.

Left: With Mark Kennedy.

Right: (From left), Rex Bullen, me and Lobby Lloyd.

With Ian Maclagen.

The Australian cover of *So Lucky* — 1981.

The American cover of the same album. (*Squint and Pout*) — 1981.

'*Sing Mammy!*' Steve McLean, the director of my shows at Kinselas — 1988.

With my beautiful best friend, Mark Hunter — 1988.

With the band during the making of *Difficult Woman* in Los Angeles.
From left: John Molo, Marty Greb, me, Paul Kelly, Terry Becker, Johnny Lee Schell
and Jimmy Haslip — 1991.

cut-up tootsies. I also had to hire a make-up person and pay him heaps of money to cover the bruises on my face. I was in agony with those shoes on, singing 'Stares and Whispers' and trying to look like I was enjoying myself. This particular time I was also asked to co-host the show with Ian Meldrum. Molly, me and a heroin hangover.

The next time I overdosed was at someone's house in Sydney in the early eighties. Paramedics had to be called. I woke up having been revived and they'd already gone. Humiliating, but relatively uneventful.

The third and last time was in a house in Melbourne, and this time I really learned my lesson. It was just a one-off occasion ... I hadn't done it for quite a few months and, even though the people I usually did it with were not around, I decided to have some heroin on my own for the first time ever. I called the only number I had in my address book under 'boo-boo'. And so, like the pizza man, twenty minutes later my order arrived.

I really had to beg the dealer to administer it for me. (I still couldn't do it myself.) He kept telling me that this was quite a strong batch and wondered if I could handle it. After assurances that I had quite a tolerance and there would be no problems, finally he was convinced.

I felt fine. I was walking down my hallway, ushering him out ... and the next thing I remember was lying on the floor being revived by paramedics, and the dealer, normally calm, cool and collected, was sweating and looking incredibly shaken.

His presence there shocked me more than anything. Drug dealers are usually gone — out the door and in their car, driving off before you can bat an eyelid. But this guy had heard me slump against the door as he left and came back and tried to revive me for a while, to no avail. Finally, he called the paramedics and stayed until they came.

If not for him I'd be dead. I'll always be grateful for that.

The paramedics gave me a lecture and I remember lying there thinking how dusty and dirty my bedroom floor was. *Don't look in there*, I said, as they were giving me the Narcan. 'You've got more important things to worry about than your floor, my girl. Do you use a lot?' *No, no, I'm Renée Geyer. I do this every now and again. It's research …*

In my euphoria I was playing this part, thinking they were going to believe me. The bizarre thing is, I think they did. They scolded me like a little kid, but I insisted that I only dabbled. Yeah, I'd been dabbling for years.

You sink into a deep depression when you're coming down after one of these episodes because you realise how close you've come to death. If no-one's around to help you, you're dead.

That last time was it for me.

Now that heroin doesn't feature in my life anymore, I look back with embarrassment at the madness of the situations I got myself into. To leave this world that way, with such 'slip o' the wrist' stupidity and no rhyme or reason, is senseless. There's something really moronic about it.

I was never addicted to heroin, thank God. My singing always saved me. I never performed well on stage while on drugs, so I mainly did it when I had days off. If I had a show the next day, or if I had a pretty heavy schedule, I couldn't indulge. It was not my incredible willpower or balance that saved me, but my job. There's also my Jewish background, which is very pragmatic and no-nonsense … and I never liked the person I became when I was 'out of it'.

I always made my own decision to take drugs; no-one had to talk me into it. When I was very young, there were people around me doing it, but no-one was saying, 'Have some of this.' It was almost always me asking for some.

When you have taken heroin in your life you can always spot the 'devil eyes' of another user a mile away. Pupils shrink to tiny dots. That's why it's called being 'pinned' – the pupils are like pinheads. If the person has got blue eyes, you only see the blue. It's quite a beautiful sight, if a scary one. Brown-eyed people can sometimes get away with it, but I can always tell.

I never went on the hunt for drugs. I always 'sent out' for them. My recollection is of always being impatient. They could never get back quick enough for me. I'd given them my money, they were going to score and they weren't back yet. Where were they? It might have only been three minutes since they were gone, but it seemed like three hours. This is what you became. Nothing else mattered.

There is nothing glamorous about the heroin scene. It's a very anti-social drug. It starts social while the hunt is on and during the ritual of taking it. But then a lot of it is just sitting there with your eyes closed, nodding off. You're not exactly stimulating company. The only glamorous moment is fleeting; the very short time you're high. The rest of the time is angst – looking for it, and then feeling sick after it. There are no redeeming features about heroin. It's a devil of a drug.

As I said before, you never do as good a job on stage stoned as when you're 'straight'. You might have interesting notions when you're high, but your delivery is not as good. Playing and singing are motor skills and they're impaired in that state. Those poor little 'interesting notions' don't even see the light of day.

I know guys like Charlie Parker and Miles Davis were wild heroin men in their heydays and that they were amazing musicians through it all. I wonder, though, how much more amazing they might have been without the drugs.

I never wanted my band to partake while we were on the road. I didn't care what musicians did after the show, but I didn't want them to be high during a show.

One gig that I did in the early eighties is particularly memorable to me because of a certain keyboard player in my band at the time. He was late for the show. We all knew where he was – he was out scoring. He'd never missed a gig before, but this night he was late. So we just went on without him.

He arrived in the middle of the first song and in his 'out of it-ness' I guess he thought that I might not notice that he hadn't been there if he crept on stage and just magically appeared at the keyboard – that I'd think, *Oh, you must have been there all the time! I just didn't see you!* So there he was, creeping to his keyboard behind me, just as I was taking a step back to sing a big note. I tripped over him ... for the whole audience to behold. This knucklehead, trying so hard to avoid me, draws more attention to the situation and causes me for the first time in my life to fall over on stage ... How in trouble was *he*?! He got to his keyboard with me looking daggers at him, all the while carrying on with the show. Two songs later I looked over and saw that from his wrists down he was going nuts, 'Fred Flintstone' fingers overplaying as usual, with more notes to the bar than you could poke a stick at – but from the wrist up he was comatose. His eyes were closed and from his mouth came a trickle of saliva that went all the way down to the keyboard. In the shimmering light it looked like a silver thread. He was so stoned.

America was cocaine. When you went to parties in LA there was always an elite spot where people would go and the door was shut behind them. You really wanted to be in that room – usually the bathroom. You didn't necessarily want the drugs, you just wanted to be invited into that secret room. Being part of that group in the bathroom meant that you were sort of special. That was more fun for me than even the drugs. I saw so many bathrooms in LA.

You could *live* in one of those rooms, they were always so elaborate. Americans are quite prissy about their bathrooms. They love to show off their fluffy designer towels and scented candles and millions of perfume bottles. Also potpourri. They love potpourri, usually with a sort of sickly-sweet fake-rose smell. And of course there are the tinted mirrors and dimmed lights so everyone looks fabulous. (Pathetic, but fabulous.)

I had many a lost weekend in America. It would start with a party, and then those elite final gatherers would adjourn to the bathroom. Even when everybody else was gone they would still be in there. They didn't need to be any more, but there they stayed, being elite and fabulous.

Those parties could turn into three-day marathons if you weren't careful. Coke. (High. Speedy.) Alcohol. (Calm down a bit.) Marijuana. (Make it a little interesting.) O-oh! Maybe a little *too* interesting! Alcohol. (Calm down again.) Coke. Drink. Smoke. Cokedrinksmokecokedrinksmokecokedrinksmoke *@!%?# ... and on and on. You'd be in search of that nirvana that you believed the perfect balance of alcohol, cocaine and marijuana could give you. It was the layering of all these things, always in the attempt to reach that tiny window of time that is mental euphoria, that mattered so much. You did reach it, over and over again, but only for such a fleeting moment that you'd immediately be in pursuit of it again. *That* is a cocaine binge.

When you're on one of these binges you become a raconteur. You become provocative. You become very confident. I convinced people at parties in America that I was a person I'm actually not. And then, thankfully, I'd never see them again. To this day they must be wondering, 'Who the hell was that girl?' I could never have been that audacious when I was straight. But you also go from that fearless high to a crashing thud on the floor of emptiness, and incredible fear and anxiety takes over. Cocaine can drop you in one second flat. It's like you've gone twenty-three floors down in a falling elevator. And that's where all the other drugs come into it, because you want to fix that feeling immediately by knocking yourself out so you *don't* feel that feeling. You're very afraid. When you've finished all your other drugs and you get to that low, it's horrible. There were times after a binge on coke that I had to drive home in the morning with no sunglasses into the blaring Californian sun, paranoid and low, anxious and guilty. I'd get home and just lie in my bed, curled up in the foetal position. Somehow I'd fall asleep, but until I did, it was the worst feeling in the world.

Marijuana made me paranoid, especially if it was very strong. I once went up on stage in the very early seventies after a really big joint, and thinking to myself, *Oh my God – my right hand! They're all staring at my right hand! Should I snap my fingers? If I snap my fingers it'll be too obvious. OK, maybe I should not snap my fingers.* My hand then became this stiff thing, not even part of my body. This was all going on while I was singing some supposedly laid-back soul number ... Then it was my foot. And then, *Oh my God! Now they're looking at my right eye. I shouldn't twitch.*

I was never much good with marijuana.

My only experiences with LSD happened back when I moved into my first home away from home. It was in Bondi and I was sharing with three girls – Chrissie, Heather and Robbie. I remember I was tripping for about fourteen hours. That was when I found out about the stomach-aches you get with LSD, because of the strychnine. A lot of LSD was laced with speed.

A whole bunch of us went to the Royal Easter Show one time and my weak bladder, which I thought I had got under control back in my school days, played up again. I had one of my laughing fits in this 'barrel ride'. One barrel rotated one way and another the other way, making it very hard to walk through. You ended up falling over and laughing. I laughed so hard trying to go through the barrel that I actually pissed myself. I thought the wee-wee was going around the barrel and I was there trying to tell people, *Get out of the barrel, it's wee-wee!* In my LSD head it was Niagara Falls. When we finally did get out of the barrel, all I had was a tiny little wet spot on my backside, which I covered with a coat around my waist for the rest of the day.

I also remember wandering around that show and imagining that people looked like something right out of *Deliverance*, with their eyes really close together – weird-looking farm-type people who reminded me of the scene in that movie where they made those guys squeal like pigs.

What I remember most about tripping on LSD was being not in reality. *Am I really alive and here, or is this just something I'm watching?* Oh yeah, and of staring for hours at my hand, which had become this psychedelic throbbing painting. I also remember LSD as being the only high that I wished would end much quicker than it ever did.

Once I joined bands my LSD days were over. No more greasy kids' stuff.

In the early seventies at the Whisky-A-Go-Go, that notorious Sydney nightclub, we used to do five sets a night. Forty minutes on, twenty minutes off. I remember the guys that ran the club would work us really hard. In the height of summer they used to turn the airconditioning off on purpose so people would get incredibly dehydrated and thirsty and buy more drinks. If that was the condition the audience was in, imagine what it was like for the band! Once, even Harry Brus, my bass player, collapsed. Our job was really punishing but we all took it like troopers, because we loved it.

In the breaks Harry and I would go down to one of the little rooms at the bottom of the stairs near the entrance for a trip into 'adventure substance land'. There used to be this guy who came to the Whisky who'd bring Moroccan hash one night, Sumatran grass the next. This particular time the guy had brought hash oil. Harry and I had some before going back up to do the next set. We were high as kites.

I remember the band starting and Harry and I looking at each other, wondering whether we'd get through the set. We were starting to see things. All of a sudden, through the front door which was straight ahead of us, what appeared to be giant bull ants were coming in. They were so big that one by one they had to bend down to get under the door, which was by no means small. I looked around at the rest of the band, but no-one else seemed perturbed – they were just carrying on with their musical business. Harry and I just kept looking back at the door and at each other, both of us becoming very pale, and very scared. It seemed like we were the only two people witnessing this Martian invasion. There must have been at least fifteen of these gigantic stick-like bull ants lowering themselves into the nightclub and standing there, just staring at us. I don't know if I was even singing or if Harry was playing the bass. It was like time froze.

Little by little, as the hash oil settled down, things started to become clearer; the blood started coming back into our heads. Now we realised that what we had thought were giant bull ants were actually the Harlem Globe Trotters! Tall, skinny and with *huge* Afros. They were touring at that time and had been told there was a funk band playing at the Whisky. Here they were, coming to check us out. It was one of the weirdest nights I've ever had.

Drugs were always around, all my life, but believe it or not, apart from the couple of close calls I've told you about, I always kept my drug taking under control. I always felt so bad afterwards that eventually it caused me to stop. I've had some very reckless friends, though. One in particular became very ill and we were all so shocked because he had been beating the odds for so long. He was someone who had taken so many chances with drugs but had never suffered drug-related illnesses. His heart was great, his skin was clear. Then one day he became very very ill – unrelated to drugs – and when the doctors had to administer medicine to try to cure him, that's when all his vital organs decided, no, they'd been holding him up long enough. They collapsed because of all the fighting they'd had to do for the last thirty years.

This was a good lesson for me. There but for the grace of God ...

My boyfriend through the seventies at first only dabbled with drugs and used to give me quite a hard time for indulging in the way I did.

Then one day I came back from one of my trips to America and there he was, using, completely immersed. All his veins were pitted. He was much further gone than I had ever been. He had always been a quiet, strong, honourable, can-do sort of guy, and overnight he had become a junkie. Eventually, after we'd been apart for a few years, he turned into this person who rolled an old lady in a milk bar and beat her up for her cash. He's spent the last fifteen years or so in and out of gaol – unbelievable to all of us who knew him. He used to be quite a hero.

This is something that I find hard to reconcile with myself. Here was someone I adored and who was so responsible and organised at the time I met him. Even though we were both introduced to drugs at the same time we took such different paths, and I can't help but feel a bit responsible for how things have turned out for him. Life for us in the seventies was so careless and without regard for the future.

I saw him once. He was driving a cab and I looked over from my car and got the shock of my life. Here was this grey, skinny guy. His eyes were lifeless and he didn't look well at all. You could see that the life had been drained out of him. He used to be such a strong, handsome, athletic kind of boy.

He, meanwhile, was probably looking over at me and thinking, *Oh my God! Look how fat she got!* I would have loved to have been somewhere overlooking that scene – two cars stopped side by side at the lights, and two people looking at each other with thought clouds mushrooming over their heads, incredulous that they could ever have been with one another. We had both become so different, in every way. That scene personified for me how different life was now.

We nodded at each other, and when the lights turned green, drove off in opposite directions.

Chapter 8

AMERICA: SO LUCKY

I was champing at the bit to get to America. The thought of making records there was not, *Could I? Can I?* It was, *Wait till they get a load of me!* I was sure I would be better accepted there than in Australia.

And so, towards the end of 1976 when I landed in LA, my head was spinning at the thought of what I was about to do. I had been signed to a deal with Polydor Records and my project was to be overseen by Hank Crosby, head of Black A&R. He had heard the 'Ready to Deal' album and had loved it, and so I got signed to a deal for America to make my next two albums.

Frank Wilson was chosen to produce me. Frank was a Motown stalwart and had produced the Temptations and Diana Ross. He was a beautiful-looking black man, and from the moment he heard my voice he was confounded. 'You're going to have a really interesting life,' he said. 'Nobody who looks like you sounds like you.'

Frank Wilson wasn't the first person in my life to say this. Ever since I was very young I'd been told I sounded like a black American singer. The fact that I'm a white Australian/Hungarian Jew has come as a bit of a shock to some people. It baffles me too.

My Jewishness might explain the way I sound. I think it has something to do with an ancient tribal culture that black people share with Jews. If you listen to a Jewish person praying in a synagogue, it's not unlike an old blues or spiritual song that one might hear in a black church. It's a kind of wailing, often very mournful. I'm not an expert on this, but these sounds might have something to do with the suffering both races have endured through centuries of hardship and then handed down through the generations and bestowed on some people unknowingly.

I am a recipient of this 'gift'. And when it comes to people I admire complimenting me on my voice, I never know what to say. I always felt like someone who has the Hope Diamond but has no idea how it got there.

We started recording what eventually became 'Moving Along' (the album with 'Stares and Whispers' on it) at Crystal Studios in Los Angeles. The studio was owned by Stevie Wonder. He'd be there at night working on his stuff while we were there all day. I remember arriving one morning and Stevie was still there from the night before. I was so nervous, but Frank Wilson insisted that we meet. All I could think of in my panic was that Stevie, being blind, would only remember shaking my clammy hand. When he asked how I was doing, the only thing that came out was this Aussie cockatoo response: *Really good, thanks ... when are you coming to Australia?*

On that album the engineer and I were the only two white people. I remember that instead of there being an instant connection, we both eyed each other very cautiously, maybe each thinking that the other was a bit of an imposter, just wanting to hang out with black folk. We sorted it out later on, but at the start it was cold.

On the first day of recording, everyone was there: the songwriters, the arrangers. The musicians were a mixture of Rufus and Stevie Wonder's backing band. I couldn't believe it. They were nice enough but aloof. They didn't know me from a bar of soap; this was just another session that Frank Wilson had booked them on.

I'd only met Frank a couple times prior to recording, so I wasn't yet feeling like I could hide under his wing. I was twenty-three, shy, scared. But this was my dream, and I kept reminding myself of it. To play with these people was *the greatest*.

They set up and tuned their instruments. There was a little glass booth for me to sing in. The first track we cut was 'Heading in the Right Direction' (one of the only songs to be re-recorded from 'Ready to Deal'). It sounded amazing to me, but there was no reaction from the guys in the band. Some of them were smiling, but I didn't know if they were smiling at the sound of their own instruments (they sounded *so* beautiful) or if they were smiling at how I was singing. But then we had a coffee break and I was completely overwhelmed by their reaction. They welcomed me with open arms, literally. Hope Diamond stuff. *Man! Where'd you learn to throw down like that? Australia? Really? You must have gone to church down there, girl!*

I couldn't wait to call everyone at home and tell them.

The biggest compliment I received from this band was yet to come. I should explain a little about the recording process first. Usually you sing a guide vocal with the band to get a backing track down. Sometimes, if the microphone and the booth are prepared for the sound to be good enough for a final vocal, then you might use the vocals as is. But most of the time the guide vocal is just to give the band an idea of the dynamics of the song. Frank Wilson was one of those people who always wanted to re-do the vocals anyway. He wanted them perfect. Later, when you're re-doing your vocals, the producer and engineer are in the control room where all the knobs are and you're out there in the main studio with the microphone, looking back through a soundproof window.

With this scene in your head, imagine the situation with me out there singing the final vocal on 'Heading in the Right Direction'. Very rarely do bands hang around to hear final vocals; after getting their cheque, they're usually out of there. But these guys stayed. It was quite a compliment. The lights in the control room were very dim and the people in this particular band were all very dark. I remember singing and not knowing how I was going until I saw teeth. One, two, three, four sets of teeth. Smiling. *Phew!*

This was serious record making. There was no mucking around. Ten a.m. start with Winchell's Donuts and coffees, then straight to tracking, with overdubs in the afternoon. Very regimented. I had never thought of music in a nine-to-five way before, but it worked.

As well as being a record producer, Frank Wilson was also a Baptist preacher. He had his own congregation and he had a choir. I was always asking him if I could join. If I sounded *so* soulful, I'd say to him, could I *please* join the choir? OK, so I wasn't into Christ. Maybe I could sing about Moses? How about it, Frank? He said no, that everybody in his choir had to be like-minded.

A little later I was dating James Jamison Jr, the son of the great bass player James Jamison Sr (James Sr was one of the most legendary bass players of all time, having played on almost all of the great Motown records). James Jr took me to a Baptist church in downtown LA where the Reverend James Cleveland, Andre Crouch, Martha Reeves and a whole host of other amazing gospel artists were singing. James Sr was playing bass in the band, and Frank Wilson was there too. I remember feeling uplifted by the amazing music, and at the same time feeling small and inadequate surrounded by all these big, beautiful, fan-waving, swooning men and women. That's when it really hit me that Frank was right: it wasn't enough to just be soulful by accident. To sing this stuff properly you truly had to believe in what you were singing about. And that's why, to this day, I don't do gospel albums. To me it would be blasphemy.

Back to the album.

I insisted on having a bit of my musical identity on that record by bringing over Barry Sullivan and Mal Logan. The record company indulged me with my Australian musos, but they weren't happy about it. Mal and Barry didn't play on much of the album, but the tracks they did play on sounded great. I'm glad that I'd stuck to my guns.

For about a month, Barry, Mal and I stayed at the Wilshire Hotel. We were in an incredible three-bedroom apartment.

Each bedroom had its own en-suite, and the living area was huge and open like the apartments I'd only ever seen on American TV. Gladys Knight's 'Pips' were staying there, as was the comedian Freddy Prinz from TV's 'Chico and the Man'. A regular on the Johnny Carson 'Tonight Show', Prinz was red-hot at the time, but apparently very wild. He used to have parties next door to us – women, alcohol, drugs – day and night. We all thought it was very exciting and very 'Hollywood', but one night, at about four in the morning, we heard noises that we initially thought were more partying. Barry Sullivan put his head out the window and shouted to keep the noise down. It turned out that the noise was Freddy Prinz blowing his head off.

The next morning the police and the press surrounded the building. Barry, Mal and I were numb with shock. It was so sad. We were on the news that night as up-and-coming rock stars from Australia commenting on Freddy Prinz. It was surreal: we'd never even met him.

When the record was finished, 'Heading in the Right Direction' came out as the first US single, and black radio all across eastern America embraced it, thinking I was a black artist. Polydor suggested not putting my photo on the cover of the album, as they were concerned it might alienate the black programmers. I was adamant. *No, this is me. I'm white, Australian, Jewish and proud. Put me on the cover.*

They did, and as soon as the radio people saw the cover they stopped playing the record.

This was in the days before the likes of Hall and Oates, George Michael and 'blue-eyed soul singers' in general were welcomed on black radio. My sound caused a lot of confusion: black people were hailing it, but being white got in the way; and white people simply didn't know what to do with me because I sounded too black.

That's what happened in America, at any rate. When 'Stares and Whispers', the first single off the album, was first heard in Australia, and then the album itself came out, people were very impressed. No Australian had put out such a sophisticated R'n'B record before.

My next trip to America was to record 'Winner' in 1977, again with Frank Wilson. This time I took Tim Partridge on bass, Greg Tell on drums and Mark Punch on guitar. Both times, bringing my own musicians created problems with my American label, but again I insisted, and the blend of the two styles of musicians worked for me.

For the duration of the making of this next album we stayed at the Chateau Marmont. This great old Hollywood hotel had a policy of keeping its guests as sheltered as possible. There were many famous people staying there, and if any of them wanted to have an extra-marital tryst every now and then, the Chateau Marmont could be trusted to keep things private and comfortable. Once, when this old English Shakespearian actor and his secret girlfriend swam in the pool that our bungalows shared, we were asked by the management to wait until they'd gone before we had our dip. Very civilised, we thought. A typical day at this hotel could be anything from seeing Lauren Hutton sunbaking nude in the garden to running into Robert DeNiro at reception. DeNiro's one of those people who, if he catches you looking at him, makes a rude face. Unfortunately, I'm like that too. So I made a face back. This went on for a few minutes till the receptionist broke it up and we both had to laugh at the silliness of it all.

During the making of 'Winner' we met some formidable musicians. It was an interesting time musically in LA, long before those clinical, technical whizzes from Toto took over the session world. There were musicians like Abe Laboriel on bass, Harvey Mason on drums and a lot of Latin players working gigs like The Baked Potato in North Hollywood. This was fiery, soulful stuff. We used go to The Baked Potato most nights after recording. One day, after hearing Abe Laboriel the night before, I asked Frank Wilson if we could get him to play on a track on the album. Sure enough, next day, there he was.

Jaco Pastorius from Weather Report and Flora Purim from Chic Chorea's band also came to visit us. They'd heard about us through The Baked Potato grapevine. Jaco invited us down to a Weather Report session, and on one of their tracks we did hand claps. I remember standing in a circle around the microphone with the legendary Weather Report and thinking, *Wait till the folks back home hear about this!* The keyboard player, Joe Zawinul, was right opposite me. He was a short guy, and every time he spoke to me he couldn't get past my breasts. He was mesmerised. I kept trying to lower myself to his eye level, but he just kept going lower. I don't think he ever saw my face. If we ever met again I think I'd have to flash my boobs and say, *Remember me?*

Never more than at this time in America did I recognise the huge difference in the black/Latin body language and the Aussie 'beauty-mate' mannerisms that we had. One day Ray Burgess (one-time Australian rock-TV show host for 'Flashes') came to do an interview with me at Crystal Studios. The drummer on the session that day was Raymond Pounds, the very laid-back drummer for Rufus. Observing the two of them meet that day was like watching a split-screen movie. On one side of the picture was Raymond Pounds, moving and talking in slow motion and extending his hand and saying, *Hooowe ya'all dooooin?* On the other side was this sped-up birdlike creature with a high voice and a nervous handshake, saying, *Yeh, how ya goin?* Ray Burgess's outfit helped too. Back in Australia it was the Bay City Rollers craze, and I guess he was a fan because he wore a tartan scarf, knee-high culottes and platform Herman Munster shoes. The look on Raymond Pound's face was priceless.

During the making of this second record for Polydor, between recording it and mixing it things changed at the record company. The head of the company got the sack and so everyone under him went too. Everything fell like a house of cards. There was no more money, so Frank Wilson was out of the picture too. The deal with Polydor fell through, and through Mushroom's negotiations we somehow ended up with the tracks and mixed them back in Sydney.

It wasn't one of my better albums. 'Winner' was a bit of a loser, I'm afraid.

On those early visits to America I was always impatient to get home and show people what I'd bought. In the seventies you could buy things in LA you just couldn't get in Australia, like jeans with really beautiful patchwork, and American-Indian turquoise jewellery. People were wearing sunglasses with their initials in diamantés. I couldn't wait to get a pair of those! Most of all, though, I couldn't wait for people to hear the records I would bring home by the suitcaseful – all the R'n'B stuff that never reached Australia.

In America I was always with people I trusted, people who I'd met through music. I never felt scared, except on one occasion. Venetta Fields, one of the background singers I became friends with on the sessions for 'Stares and Whispers', took me to meet Ike Turner at his notorious Bollock Studios. The door opened, and Ike greeted me by putting a hash pipe in the shape of a penis in front of my face. *Hi, suck on this!* His rooms were furnished like an old American saloon bordello – lots of dark maroon crushed velvet cushions on big overstuffed leather couches and ashtrays in the shape of people fucking. Ike was also fond of twirling his gun around his finger. This was the first time I'd ever seen a gun close up. I had thought I was a woman of the world, but this reduced me to a scared little shnook who wanted her mummy.

I thought Ike was quite funny, though, and lonely too. It was just after his split with Tina Turner that Venetta took me to meet him. He didn't want to let us go – he wanted to jam. I was tugging at Venetta's sleeve, *I wanna go now.* We ended up staying there for about an hour and a half, I guess; I'm not sure. What with the gun twirling and the hash pipe, I was in a bit of a daze. Legend had it there used to be hole in the roof of the control room of Ike's studio with a gun pointed down on the console at whoever the poor producer or engineer was at the time. I guess if Ike didn't like what he heard, *Boom boom*. I saw that hole.

Those early visits to the States were the beginning of my love affair with American food. You'd get these huge plates heaped high, and in the beginning you'd feel guilty, wondering how people in the Third World were coping. You'd say to yourself *Oh! The waste! I could never finish all this*. It didn't take long, though, before I started finishing everything in sight. My weight problems started on those trips.

Americans have the knack for great food presentation too. I'm sure they inject their fruits and vegetables with something to make them bigger and brighter. The apples are redder, the grapes are greener and the carrots are *really* orange. A lot of the time you're eating rubbish, but it looks so fuckin' good ... It conned me every time.

Going home after my visits to the States became harder each time. I was starting to develop some really good friendships and I loved the life over there. I knew that eventually I was going to make a more permanent move to America.

While making 'Winner' I became friendly with Rob Fraboni, who I'd met a few years earlier when he toured Australia with Joe Cocker after producing the 'Stingray' album with him. Rob and Joe heard 'Ready to Deal' and became fans. I'd always wanted to make a record with Rob producing, so when the opportunity arose in 1979, the idea for 'So Lucky' (the album) was born.

Rob took me under his wing. He introduced me to the guys in The Band, and to some great musicians who were playing with Eric Clapton at the time. I'd already met some of them a few years back when I toured as support for Clapton in Australia. My favourites were Carl Radle, the bass player and Marcy Levy, one of the backing singers (she's now a very successful solo artist and songwriter in England and she goes by the name of Marcella Detroit).

Rob Fraboni lived in a beautiful two-storey loft in a big chateau which used to be a sort of safe house for young actresses in the thirties and forties. Katharine Hepburn, Bette Davis and the like had stayed there while making their movies. The house was called La Fontaine because of its huge fountain in the front courtyard, and it was right in the middle of West Hollywood. The apartment had a magnificent staircase and high ceilings with beautifully handcarved

Spanish-style wooden beams holding it up. It was like Auntie Mame's New York apartment. I went to many a great party in that beautiful place and drank lots of tequila, which seemed to be the favourite beverage in those days. I remember a little guest toilet near the front door which overlooked the fountain. I was in there so often, fixing my make-up, trying to keep myself looking decent – the parties went on for hours – and I'd always be thinking how fantastic the apartment was, and how great it would be to live in it one day.

Years later, long after Rob had moved out, I got that apartment. I didn't have much money for anything else, but I managed to pay the rent on that place for three years and I adored it. And every time I would go into that guest toilet I would get this kinda drunken tequila feeling, remembering my earlier times there.

In the early stages of 'So Lucky', when Rob and I were workshopping and doing demos, we recorded a version of 'I Think I'm Going Out Of My Head' with saxophonist David Sanborn, who'd played with Stevie Wonder, The Rolling Stones and James Taylor, and Richard Tee, who was one of the great soul piano-playing accompanists of all time. Richard used to play with the Voices of East Harlem and he'd backed Aretha Franklin and Roberta Flack.

One night Richard gave me a ride back to Hollywood from the studio in Malibu. On the way home he wanted to smoke a cigarette. He had this cigarette lighter in the shape of a gun, a horrible-looking thing. The lighter was in the front pocket of his jeans, and his jeans were very tight. In trying to extract the lighter from his pocket he had the car weaving all over the Pacific Coast Highway. To an onlooker it would have appeared that a drunk was at the wheel, and sure enough, the LAPD stopped us. Richard whispered, *Don't say anything leave it to me*. I remember the policeman being rude and patronising.

I never thought I'd really see the redneck cop you see in the movies, but here he was. He was looking at me and asking if I was OK, as if he felt sorry for me because I was with Richard, this black man. When he gave Richard some forms to fill out, he asked, 'Can you read and write?' I was so disgusted I cried out, *Do you know who this man is?* Richard kicked me, trying to shut me up. He knew full well that none of this helped when a black man faces a redneck policeman in America.

The crazy thing was, Richard actually had some cocaine in one of his pockets and the cop never even searched him. He was more concerned with the fact that Richard was black and I was white. He put Richard in gaol for the night for reckless driving.

That night was quite an adventure. Richard Tee was a big, sweet, gentle man and one of the greatest R'n'B keyboard players ever. Unfortunately, he died of cancer a few years ago.

Also around this time, Rob Fraboni introduced me to Ricky Fataar, a great drummer. He was from South Africa and was in a famous R'n'B band at the time with Blondie Chaplin, called the Flames. They were one of the first soul bands to come from there to the West. In 1972, Ricky and Blondie joined the Beach Boys and played on the 'Holland' album (which was recorded in Holland). Ricky became my collaborator and we were quite close. To this day I have huge respect for him. At the time, he, with Rob producing, was making an album with Ian McLagan (ex-Faces) and his Bump Band, consisting of Ian, Ricky, Johnny Lee Schell and a

Japanese bass player called Ray Ohara. They were doing their album at Shangri-La, The Band's old home and studio. (It was where they filmed *The Last Waltz*, directed by Martin Scorsese.) Rob suggested I have a sing with the Bump Band to see what would happen. We hit it off and it seemed right to choose this band to play on my album. They were R'n'B musicians, but more 'rocky' than I'd been used to before, and at the time it was the best thing for me.

Also at that time Bonnie Raitt was recording with the Bump Band and there was this little community at Shangri-La. When Bonnie was on the road I would stay in the guest bungalow, and likewise when I was away she'd do the same. These people became like family. To this day, Bonnie and those guys are my good friends. The guitar player Johnny Lee Schell is my dearest music friend in America.

Ian 'Mac' McLagan is an adorable, funny character. He's remained exactly the same throughout his career, from the Small Faces, to the Faces, to his own solo thing, back with Rod Stewart, and so on. He's got the most incredible sense of humour. He's like a pixie, like some ancient good imp. Every time I'm around him I have good fortune in my life. Mac wrote the song 'So Lucky'. He's also one of the greatest Hammond organ players around.

When I was very young, I never had much time for the girlfriends or wives of band members. I considered them wasted space. I used to think that most of them lived through their partners. As I've gotten older and, I hope, wiser, I realise that that is more the exception than the rule. A lot of the wives and girlfriends of the musicians I've worked with are clever, self-contained women who are sometimes more fun to be with than their mates.

That's what I found with the Bump Band.

Ricky Fataar was married to Penelope Tree, the famous London model from the sixties and seventies, who had been photographer David Bailey's paramour for a while. Ricky and Penelope were good friends to me in those LA days. I really liked Penelope. She is a very intelligent, beautiful girl with a good heart. Originally from a well-to-do family, she has a bohemian soul. She and Ricky have split up now, but I still think about her.

Ian McLagan's wife, Kim, is a peaches-and-cream English beauty. She too has a heart of gold. She's like something out of a scene from *To Sir With Love*. Kim was the girlfriend of Keith Moon of The Who and was very much abused by him. Mac rescued her from that situation and they've been together ever since. They really were meant for each other.

Johnny Lee's wife Beth is a great girl. Her grandfather was Jules Styne, one of the great broadway musical writers ('Gypsy' was one of his most famous musicals). Beth and I are both Jewish and have a lot to laugh about being Jewish Princesses in the rock'n'roll world. We're still very close.

Also through Rob I met and have remained close to Terry Becker, the engineer on 'So Lucky'. She has great natural instincts about the sound in music. In fact, she's now Professor of Studio Engineering at Boston's Berklee College of Music.

All these girls were as much a part of my happy memories of making 'So Lucky' as the boys. Recording the album was a nurturing, warm experience. I met a lot of great musicians on that record – Willie Smith, the organ player, Bobby King, the great singer who was with Ry Cooder, James Ingram (who at that time was still a keyboard player doing a little bit of singing) and Rick Danko, The Band's bass player. Joe Cocker also jammed with us, but not much happened due to a bottle of Jim Beam.

Because I was still signed to them, Mushroom ended up financing the 'So Lucky' album and later secured a deal with Portrait in the US. It became an Australian project being done in America. Ricky Fataar was really co-producer on that record, because he sourced most of the songs with me and helped arrange them. Fraboni's gift was putting us together, and being a good overseer.

One night I was having dinner at Ricky's house. He was a big Eddie Grant fan and he played me one of his records. When 'Say I Love You' came on we both immediately thought that it would be great to do.

Song ideas came to me from all over the place. I heard the Lee Michaels song 'Do You Know What I Mean' on the car radio and brought it up to Rob. We recorded that in the early hours of one morning, in one take. I remember that it was the height of summer. While we were playing, the back doors of the studio were open and the sky was red from bushfires.

All the band were bringing me ideas. Rob brought me the Howard Tate song 'You Don't Know Nothin' About Love'. *Had to do that!* I wrote 'Good Lovin'' with Mac and some of the other guys in the band. Mac gave me his song 'So Lucky', and he also brought me 'I Can Feel the Fire', which Ronnie Wood from the Rolling Stones wrote. The Allan Toussaint song 'On The Way Down', which Lowell George made famous with Little Feat, we did almost as a jam: it was done in one take at about two in the morning, and you can actually hear the beginning of it start up out of nothing, with Ricky just counting it in. We layered the background vocals on it later.

'Say I Love You' came out in Australia in June 1981 as a single while we were still finishing the album. On my twenty-eighth birthday, on September 11, it reached number one in Sydney. It was a happy day. It was also the day that James Ingram, Bobby King and Willie Smith came to Shangri-La to do the background vocals for 'On The Way Down'. The co-engineer, Tim Kramer, was a big fan of theirs too. He and I had been rehearsing what we'd say to them, who'd ask them what they wanted to eat or drink and who was going to make the sandwiches. We were planning all this stuff like two children waiting for Mickey Mouse to arrive. When they finally came we did an about-face and tried to act all cool – the opposite of what we were feeling. They must have thought we were unfriendly. But believe me, we were pumped.

During 'So Lucky' we knew we were making something really special. People were dropping in all the time. They'd been hearing about this record and my singing and wanted to check it out. I was still a bit shy, and all this attention was quite bewildering. I just said thank you a lot.

Every time we layered the songs with any overdubs it was always a very good experience. And there weren't a lot of overdubs; most of the record was made live with the band. This was a whole new way of recording for me, and once again I learned so much from the making of this album.

I also learned that a lot of the recording sessions were run on cocaine in those days. Ours was no exception. I found out later from Ian McLagan when he was making his record that it seemed like the drug budget came first and the recording budget second. I guess that happened on my record too.

When 'So Lucky' came out in December of 1981 in Australia, a lot of people were saying that it was very different from my other stuff, that it was more rocky. It was, and I liked it that way. Inasmuch as 'Moving Along' was a great album, it was Frank Wilson who called the shots. Back in 1975, 'Ready To Deal' had been a collaborative effort, and now so was 'So Lucky'. Everyone chipped in to make it sound the way it did.

I don't think I realised what 'Say I Love You' was going to do to my life. When Mushroom first picked it for a single I wasn't thrilled; I wasn't sure that it was a good representation of the whole album. I liked it as a song, but it wasn't much chop vocally. However, it propelled 'So Lucky', the album, to huge national success, and when I returned to Australia I played to full houses everywhere. The beauty of that album was in the sheer uplifting feeling you got when you heard it. There was no one thing that made it great; it was the sum of its parts made it a hit. My *biggest* hit.

America had done me a good turn, and in the back of my mind I knew I'd go back. Five years later America became my home.

Chapter 9

CHOOKAS

I've always been a TV junkie. As a child I loved it, mostly because I couldn't get enough. My parents didn't let me and my brothers watch it a lot, so it was always a big treat. Later, when I left home and joined a band, TV was there for company in those lonely hotel rooms.

Watching television was fabulous: the worse the show, the more riveting. Being on television, however, was a different matter. There's a famous quote from Noel Coward that goes, 'One should only ever appear on television but never watch it.' I've always thought the opposite. When I decided to be a singer, I had no idea that TV would play such a big part in my career.

The first time was in 1972 on Channel 7's 'The Bob Rogers Show' in Sydney. Someone from the programme had seen me singing with Mother Earth and asked me to come on the show. It was pretty exciting at first, the thought of singing with a fifteen-piece band who would write the arrangement for any song I wanted to sing. I picked 'Lover Come Back' (pinched from an old 'Aretha Franklin Sings Jazz' album).

I was in a daze ... I don't remember much, except being told to face the camera with the red light on top of it. At the end of my song, Bob Rogers came over and said, 'That was great.' Then, with the cameras still on us, and as the music was playing to the ad break, he said, 'Now act like we're just talking.' I didn't understand: we *were* talking. The moment the cameras stopped, his face got real serious and he walked away without another word. I was worried that I'd done something wrong, but the director said I was fabulous and that Mr Rogers simply had to go off and get ready for the next segment.

And so began my love–hate relationship with Australian television.

In my nearly three decades of appearing on TV, I've always left a television studio feeling unfulfilled and unhappy with my performance, vowing that I'd learned from my mistakes and that the next time would be better. It never was. Whether it was my hair, the make-up, my outfit or the actual performance, to me it was never any good. I used to ring my mother straight after a live-to-air TV show asking, *Was it really bad?* My mother was always the first person I'd call, because I knew she'd tell me the truth. She never thought it was *as* bad as I did, but still, not great.

This was especially true in my early days. My mother never used to like to see me on TV back then. I didn't have great entertainer skills: I could never put together the perfect mouth and hand gestures that other singers seemed to be able to do. I've always been envious of people who can *shine* on TV. Those who can make you feel they are perfectly at ease are true entertainers. Performers like John Farnham and Ricky May could sing in the middle of a haystack with a funny hat on and somehow you wouldn't think it was corny. It's as if they're in on the joke and are just going along with it, but somehow they're bigger than it.

If I had to make a weird face in order to reach a big note, there it was for everyone to see. This looked even worse when the cameras were trained to look up my nostrils. You could bet that when a big, blonde, lusty girl like me came on the scene, belting out a song with gusto like I did, they had cameras shooting from the ground up to emphasise the rawness even more, to the point of 'gorilla-ness'.

The orange make-up didn't help, either. They used the same orange foundation on everyone, regardless of skin colour. I guess it was a legacy of the black and white television days, but it sure seemed a long time before they got out of the habit of using it.

In the seventies there was one style for everybody. If it didn't work, too bad. I remember the make-up lady at the Melbourne ABC studios in Ripponlea once saying (after I insisted on doing my own make-up), 'All right then, go on looking like a fishwife . . . see if I care.'

Whenever they brought the hot rollers out, I got worried. There were some remarkable Farrah Fawcett hairdos done on me in the seventies. Live, I was sort of natural, with wild hair and only a little make-up. On TV, however, I was curled and schmurled to within an inch of my life till I looked like a drag queen.

The sets didn't do anything to put me at ease, either. Once, on Darryl Somer's 'Tonight Show', I sang a song called 'Love So Sweet', a basic little love song with very simple lyrics. When the time came to rehearse, I couldn't believe my eyes: the set was a Dali-esque extravaganza! They had built a long hallway down which I was to walk while singing the song. Along the walls were holes with people's arms poking through, some trying to grab me as I walked by, others waving saxophones about. For the life of me I couldn't work out what they were getting at. Was it something in the lyrics …?

I always dreaded doing the Tonight Shows. The producers had to come up with an hour-and-a-half show twice, and sometimes even three times a week, and there would be three or four singers on any given show in between segments with comedians, interviews with actors, the barrel and the wheel, et cetera et cetera. All of this meant that there was always pressure, and not much time for a lot of things. But come hell or high water they had sets! Bigger than Ben Hur, sometimes, and put together according to someone's vision of whatever the song was. They scared the shit out of me.

I think I often wore a kind of tortured, 'doggie-caught-doing-a-poo' expression on TV in those days. It came from a cross between trying to pretend that this all came naturally, the fact that I was forever trying to refine my facial expressions as I reached for that big note, and, last but not least, it came from me trying to stop myself looking at the monitors. You can bet that when an entertainer is not experienced they can't help looking at themselves in the monitors (the little TV screens facing the artist and depicting what's being taped). You look in there as if into a big mirror to check that you look OK. *Bad move.* If you don't like what you see, you're stuck with it:

there's nothing you can do but keep singing. Only now you have a mental picture in your head – one that you don't like – hence the doggie face. People watching at home can tell, too. You look really distracted and they must wonder why you keep looking 'over there'.

Imagine me, now, looking at myself in the monitors – seeing that orange face, the Farrah Fawcett hairdo – and being lowered from the ceiling on a half moon, getting off the moon then walking forward with smoke all around me and trying to find the camera with the red light on it . . . Oh yeah, all while singing 'Stares and Whispers'. I think that was for one of the 'Paul Hogan Show' specials.

That show was scary for me (though I loved watching it) because they had a big budget.

Big budgets were trouble. They meant bigger, even more elaborate sets, and consequently more knuckle-head performances by me. On another one of the Paul Hogan specials I sang 'Thrill is Gone', the B.B. King song. This time they decided it would be a 'living' set. They got about thirty near-naked dancers, covered them in baby oil, and had them writhing on the floor around me all through the song. (Maybe they got the idea from the 'slaves building the pyramids' kind of background vocals I had on my version: you know, Babylon, Sodom and Gomorrah . . . Who knows?)

My sex symbol image in the seventies *couldn't* have come from my TV performances. I was always awkward, unless I shut my eyes and just let myself go.

The only time TV was fun for me was on ABC shows like 'GTK' or 'Radio with Pictures'. These programmes usually screened live tapings of performances of me with my band. The cameras just captured whatever it was we were creating.

It was raw and very genuine, and for those who liked the music, it was the only way to see it.

The ABC was usually a good experience for me. They picked their musical acts carefully, and great care was taken with the sound. From 'The Norman Gunston Show' to 'The Naked Vicar Show' through to 'Roy and H.G.', the sound was given top priority – the best I've ever heard on a stage in a TV studio.

The commercial stations were another whole matter. We were part of a much bigger picture. The attitude was not, *If she looks and sounds good, we do too.* It was more about getting as much current 'hot' talent on one show as was humanly possible, and throwing it all up in the air to see what stuck with ratings the next day.

When it came to programmes like 'The Graham Kennedy Show', 'The Don Lane Show' and even 'The Mike Walsh Show' (which was a midday show), it was a bit like a circus. You'd arrive for your rehearsal, see your set and, with mouth agape, be whisked off to 'dressing room row'. There you'd sit nervously as you listened to the opera singer next door doing her scales while the acrobat two doors up practised standing on his partner's head. Meanwhile, Jeannie Little could be heard somewhere going, *Oohwaaah, daahling.* Anyway, someone would finally come and take you off for your rehearsal. That was the fun part for me. I almost always knew someone from the orchestra, and their eyes would light up when they saw me – mainly, I think, because I used to do cool songs with really challenging things for them to play. I always wished the final performance was as good as the rehearsal . . . so laid back and so much fun.

But unfortunately it was all uphill from there. Now it was time for make-up, hair and nerves. Music was never again on my mind for the rest of the time I was there. If you didn't know anyone appearing with you, you'd sort of wander around aimlessly, waiting for your three minutes of glory. Almost always, there was Bert Newton, at that time everyone's favourite sidekick, cheerful and busy, working on his outfits for a skit or the wheel segment. He'd pass you in the hallway, and he'd say, 'Chookas'. I don't actually know where this word comes from, but it means 'good luck' in the language of Australian TV. It's a very Melbourne word (I never heard it much in Sydney). It's a really sweet expression, and whenever I hear it now I remember it fondly. But at the time, it gave me the willies.

So finally it would be time for my song, and out onto the Cecil B. de Mille set I'd go. Then it would be like I'd just had the anaesthetic before the operation: 1 ... 2 ... 3 ... and it's over. It was a blur. *What happened? Was I OK? Couldn't hear myself ... hope I was in tune.* All I could remember before the blackout was the monitor – seeing myself in the fucking monitor. *Oh well, better call Mum. She'll know.*

Another memorable show from the seventies was 'Countdown'. The thing I remember the most about it was that hangdog look of Molly's. You could tell when there was some kind of drama (which was often) between him and director/producer Michael Shrimpton from the yelling and slamming of doors in and out of Molly's dressing room. It was never clear what the arguments were about, and somehow I think maybe Molly and Michael didn't know either, but they pumped Molly up. It was as if he needed them to get through the shows each week.

I had my moments on that show, too. There was always something dramatic happening when we went to Ripponlea on Saturday mornings. I was usually picked up by Ray Evans, my manager, really early in the morning. On the way we'd usually argue about something that went wrong the night before at our gig, so we'd always look a sight, storming through the doors of the studio, Ray trailing behind trying to explain something that I was not interested in hearing. We must have given people who saw us in public the impression of a haughty, bored, ungrateful prima donna and her poor, long-suffering manager.

I also had some major hangovers on that show, left over from the night before. The hardest times to deal with them were when I was a co-host and had to read out the top ten songs in the country that week. There was almost always an ABBA song on that chart, or something else I disliked. I remember trying really hard not to sound too mean when I read out the names.

Molly and I had many an argument backstage on 'Countdown'. I honestly can't remember what any of them were about. We shared the same manager, so I'm sure a lot of it was the tension created from a touch of rivalry at having the same representative.

There was one controversial episode of 'Countdown' where I slapped Molly on air. It was me and John Paul Young co-hosting with Molly in about 1975, and I slapped him after he dared me to as a sort of a joke, and then John Paul Young did too. People like to think that it was terribly dramatic and serious, but in fact it was off-the-cuff and dumb. Molly loved it; I could see his eyes light up when I did it. People ask me about it all the time, like it was this big drama. It was showbiz.

I did slap Molly for real in Michael Gudinski's office once, however. Michael was telling me to do something I didn't want to do – a TV show or something – and for some reason Molly, who was waiting to have a meeting, chipped in to the argument. I told him to mind his own business, and when he wouldn't, I slapped him. That one was for real.

Hosts of TV shows rarely had anything more than small talk in common with their musical guests. Mostly, the two couldn't be further apart as people. There was just one occasion when I had a close encounter with a TV personality. This guy would always flirt with me every time I appeared on one of his shows. I knew he liked big, buxom, blonde women, but I didn't fancy him. I'd been dared many times by friends to take him up on one of his invitations, and so, one day after being asked back to his place for the umpteenth time, I said yes.

His house was a huge mansion with mirrors everywhere, ceilings and all. We spent most of the night in the kitchen, and most of that time he talked about himself. I don't know how it got to this point – there were lots of drinks, I guess – but we ended up in the living room, and after a brief necking session he ended up completely disrobed. I remained fully clothed, sitting on the edge of the couch. During the necking, he had revealed his Oedipus complex. That was enough for me: I wanted out of there. It was about three o'clock in the morning and he gave me a funny look when I said I had to go because the band was rehearsing. *Oh, we rehearse at strange hours*. He called a private cab company to take me to my hotel, and I remember thinking that that would be the last time I'd be invited onto his show. I was wrong. I did it a few more times after that, but he never uttered another word to me.

Unfortunately, television goes hand in hand with the promotion of records, and so far they haven't invented another more effective way, visually and instantly, of making people aware of your latest song. If it was up to me, I probably wouldn't do TV at all, especially now that I'm older and self-conscious about the fact that I'm carrying much more weight than I should. But it's part of being a singer, and I still very much want to be a singer. So … *chookas*.

Chapter 10

BACK IN THE USA

Late in 1983, when I was still living in Sydney and still with Mushroom (just), I got a call in the middle of the night: 'Can you get on a plane tomorrow morning? There are tickets at the airport. Sergio Mendes wants you to audition for his band.' It was John McLain, the executive at A&M who was always looking out for me. He had put my name forward as the new lead singer for Sergio's band. 'Renée,' he continued, 'I know it's not the sort of thing that you want to do, but this will get your foot in the door.'

He was right: I wasn't crazy about the idea. I'd always thought of Sergio Mendes as a poor man's Quincy Jones. But I knew that John was right – it was a foot in the door in America – and so he convinced me.

I went to LA and was met at the airport by my close friend

Annie Wright, who was working at A&M for Mushroom at the time. We headed straight for the A&M studios. There were four other singers waiting to audition. Bruce Swedien, who'd worked on the vocals for Michael Jackson's 'Off the Wall' and 'Thriller', was the engineer. After I'd sung a bit he brought out a suitcase from the control room. He opened it up, and inside, neatly lined up, were all these gold microphones. 'Hmmm,' he muttered, as he picked out the right one for me. I knew I was in with a chance.

The song was atrocious – something like, 'I love the way you move your body'. It was an unimaginative dance ditty, but I kept hearing John McLain's words in my head: *get your foot in the door* … I learned that song and belted it out as if I really meant it. I had a sheet of paper with the words on it, and by the end of the session that piece of paper was a moist, crumpled ball in my fist.

Later that day John McLain called to say, 'I don't know what you did, but you scared the shit out of them. Sergio wants to take us to dinner tonight.'

We went to Sergio's house and we drank Crystal Champagne. Then we went to a Japanese restaurant. There was lots of saki – my first time – so I was pretty sloshed by the end of dinner. I remember Sergio saying, 'You have the posture of a warrior,' and I'm like, *I'm not worried* … John was kicking me under the table. *A warrior, not a worrier!*

Sergio wanted me to go down to Lake Tahoe the next night to see his show and decide if his band was something I could fit in with. It was a pretty corny show, and all the girl I was replacing did was sing two songs and play tambourine with a bit of back-up singing thrown in for luck. *Remember, Renée* … John McLain's words were still in my ear. *Foot in the door* …

Ah, foot shmoot! I couldn't do this.

After the show there was a little party in Sergio's suite. We agreed that we'd talk the next day, back in LA. I never heard from him again. *He knew*. Warrior or not, I just wasn't right for this job.

John never forgave Sergio Mendes. I tried to explain to him that it was just not the right thing for me, and that Sergio knew what he was doing. But John took it as an insult to him, personally.

I hung out with my buddy Annie, did some shopping and left LA three days later.

The next time I came to America it was my own decision, and I was coming over for good. In 1986, after being dropped by Warners, I was determined to make a life for myself over there.

I told my mother and close friends who were worried about me that I had work lined up. I had nothing. All I had was the name of one lawyer, Paul Schindler, who used to do all of Mushroom's American deals. A journalist friend in Sydney knew of a guy who had a loft to rent in Tribeca, down past the village near Wall Street. I took the number and that's where I went when I landed in New York.

It was a great old building, and I was getting the apartment on the top floor, which sounded fantastic. In reality, however, it was a dump. All it was was a big cement room with a cement floor, a bed, a stove, a toilet and a shower nozzle that came out of the wall – no cubicle, just a drain. But the most striking thing about this room was that in the middle of it stood a mound of dirt as high as the windows, and as wide as a quarter of the room itself. Just dirt. A big heap of soil, unexplained when I asked the landlord what the hell it was doing there (he muttered something about someone who was meant to have gotten rid of it but hadn't). He wanted $1000 a month rent from me to stay there — a lot money for a room with a big lump of dirt in it.

I stayed there for a week, just long enough to get myself another apartment in a suburb called Murray Hill, which was halfway between Soho and Uptown, in the Irish part of Manhattan. It was a nice, clean little apartment with a doorman downstairs, so I felt safe. I paid rent for three months in advance and told myself I'd start from here and see what happened. I had the phone put on, rented a television and called everyone I knew. I was starting from scratch.

Before I left Australia I'd joked with friends that, hey, the worst thing that could happen would be that I'd be a waitress by day. You know, *No. 43, Harry. Bacon and eggs. Make it snappy.* With the hat and the hankie. Of course, I'd be doing this while moonlighting as a fabulous chanteuse.

Such a romantic notion was soon dashed. I decided very quickly that I'd rather eat in a diner than work in one. I had to find some work. Amongst other things I sold pens in New Jersey on the phone, I read stories to sick people for a while, and, when things got really tough, I even sold some of my beloved chatchkas to secondhand stores in Soho. Paul Schindler, my lawyer contact, got me a little session for Jellybean Martinez, the dance producer, for which I never got paid.

'So Lucky' producer Rob Fraboni, who was living in New York at that time, threw me a bone every now and again. I did lots of demos for up-and-coming songwriters, and I did a few sessions. I sang on albums by Washington 'go-go' band Trouble Funk (including their album 'Woman of Principle'), and on Nick Tremulus's album.

Financially I always struggled in America, from the minute I got there to the day I came home. I just never had enough money. Occasionally I got a call from Australia or New Zealand to come back and do a commercial or a show somewhere. Australasia always bailed me out somehow. At one point I even did an acting job in Sydney in a short film called *A Day and a Half*, and folks, I'm definitely not an actress. This is how broke I must have been. Unqualified, here I was, starring in a movie with one of my favourite actors, Chris Haywood, having to cry and emote in ways that even Meryl Streep would have trouble with. It was really hard. I had to summon up all sorts of things, like people and animals dying, in order to cry in that film. The crying scene lasted three minutes on the screen, but kept me sad for weeks. Anyway, I got my money and went back to America ready for another battle of survival.

Despite the financial difficulties, living in New York was a constant adventure. I loved the fact that you could go see a movie, *eat*, hear a band, *eat*, see a play, *eat*, go to an art gallery, *eat* – anything you wanted, at almost any time of the day or night.

What seemed like a break came towards the end of my first year in America. There was an off-Broadway show playing down at the Village Gate in Soho with three girl singers in it. It was a tribute show to all the great sixties' pop tunes. There was a black girl who did all the Diana Ross and Tina Turner-type songs, a brunette Janis Joplin and Melanie type, and a white girl who sang Dusty Springfield and Lulu. I auditioned for the Dusty and Lulu part. There was a big cattlecall of girls going for that same part. At auditions in America people get really dolled up, thinking that that's the way the producer would want them to look. These girls were all dressed in sixties outfits, with wigs and everything. *They were serious.* I was definitely underdressed in my jeans and a T-shirt. When I was called, I sang 'You Make Me Feel Like a Natural Woman'. Towards the end of the song, I had to hold one big note, and I remember taking off my sunglasses, putting them down on the piano, belting out that note – *Oh-oh-ohhhhhh!* – and putting my glasses back on at the end. There was an embarrassingly long silence. The piano player, the director and the producer just sat there, and then finally the producer said, 'Ahem. Can you leave your information? We'll call you.' That was it.

Two months later, when I was signed to A&M Records and had gone to LA to live, they tracked me down. The director called to say, 'Congratulations you got the part.' I levelled with them. *I don't need it now. I've got a record deal.*

My chance to go and make an album in LA was due entirely to John McLain. At the time he was still at A&M and had become head of black A&R.

In New York I'd avoided calling John for as long as I could out of a sense of pride: I really thought I'd be able to do things on my own. He and I had also had rather a serious personal relationship a few years before, and it always seemed to interfere with business. But by the end of my year in New York, with not many secure prospects on the horizon, I caved in and called him.

John had always been annoyed by my career decisions. He often complained that I was a great talent but that I always did the opposite of what he thought would get me ahead. He couldn't believe that I hadn't come straight to LA for his help. He didn't understand what I saw in New York.

A meeting he had with Hamish Stuart of the now defunct Average White Band gave him an idea. He thought that putting me together with Hamish and his band – the great drummer Steve Ferrone, Neil Larson on keyboards and Anthony Jackson on the bass – would make for a great album. The idea of a band composed of a white Scotsman, a white Australian, a white American, a black Englishman and a black American, all of them amongst the best in their field, would be quite a band to behold, both live and on record.

I was a Hamish Stuart fan already. The 'Ready to Deal' album was heavily influenced by the Average White Band, and Hamish remembered me supporting them in Australia around that time. I was flown to LA. Hamish and I met up and we hit it off, so it was decided that I would join the band, called Easy Pieces.

The album we made together took forever. I was signed in early 1987 and the thing didn't see the light of day till late 1988. Los Angeles, being basically a movie town, is run by meetings. It is also a place where most people seem to be what they call 'in development'. What this means is that you have your meeting, agree on something, and then you're supposed to develop the idea further. In the movie biz you actually get paid for this. So now you're having meetings about the development of your development ... It's really producers doing this: not knowing what to do with you, but not wanting anyone else to have you till they decide what to do with you, they keep you in a kind of limbo. In Hollywood you're forever running into people who have this sort of tortured smile on their face, saying how great it is that they have a deal with someone, but that it's in development stage at the moment. This stage can last a person's whole career and still get them nowhere.

So because the music industry is based in Hollywood, some of this unfortunately has rubbed off. I too was in a kind of development hell, forever waiting for the phone to ring, forever waiting for calls to be returned. Once we'd agreed on something, I was forever waiting for the lawyers to work it out, and then finally waiting for someone to get back to town to sign something in order to get money. The actual joy and celebration of getting the deal was severely diminished by the long, drawn-out, worry-filled steps leading finally to The Cheque. (Which, let's face it, is the only thing that says the deal is done.)

The Easy Pieces album cost way too much. We ended up using three producers and recording in many different studios. There were really long breaks in between recording. Hamish had just accepted a job with Paul McCartney as bass player, and Ferrone was working with Duran Duran and then Eric Clapton as their tour drummer. While their intentions were good – this project was their baby, after all, and they tried to make it their first priority – somehow it just didn't work out that way.

There was also a lot of turmoil between Hamish's manager and Neil Larson. Neil ended up leaving, and even though he played on most of the record, on the cover there's only four of us; no Neil. Meanwhile the record company, A&M, was about to be taken over by Polygram, so 'Easy Pieces' came out without any fanfare and consequently faded away pretty quickly. A pity. It was a really good album.

While 'Easy Pieces' was being finalised I also took some extracurricular gigs. Joe Cocker's manager, Michael Lang, who was representing me at the time, put me on tour with Joe in the US and in Europe. I'd just sung a duet with him on his 'Unchain My Heart' album, on a song called 'Trust in Me'.

I was hired as background singer/special guest on the tour. I'd never been to Europe before, so it was very exciting.

Rome was the first stop on the tour, and I flew in from Australia, having just done a session in Sydney. It was the longest flight I had ever been on, and I remember it being an uncomfortable marathon. As if that wasn't enough, when I got to Rome the airline lost my luggage. The only other person whose luggage was lost from that flight was Germaine Greer. I didn't have to do too much complaining ... she took care of that. (If I'm good at kicking up a fuss in a crisis situation, Germaine Greer is formidable. I decided I could relax. As long as my luggage was with hers, I was definitely going to get it back. The poor luggage guy was a battered man by the end.)

That was an amazing trip ... Rome, Germany, France. I was surprised at the indifference of Joe's band. They'd all done it before, but I couldn't believe they could be in Rome and stay in bed until the soundcheck. I was knocking on their doors: *Isn't anyone coming with me to the Sistine Chapel?* To them it was New Jersey but to me it was *Roma*!!

I had a problem with Germany. In places like Frankfurt we'd be playing in venues where Hitler had held his rallies. Every now and again I'd look up and get a bad feeling in my stomach, thinking that fifty years ago these halls had been filled with the Nazis that were responsible for my grandparents' deaths in the gas chambers. Here I was on the very same stage, singing to the Nazis' grandchildren. I remember leaving those halls and spitting on the ground before I got on the tour bus.

It was because of 'Easy Pieces', and because I'd co-written some of the songs on that record with Hamish, that I was signed to a publishing deal with EMI Music in LA as a songwriter. Pat Lucas, the woman who signed me, is to this day one of my mentors and most loyal supporters. She'd been a fan of my records since the seventies. She signed me as a writer based on my potential. I'd co-written songs on a lot of my albums with the bands, so I'd had a bit of experience, but I was never thought of as a real songwriter. Pat thought it was a natural progression for me.

This was at a time when EMI encouraged their writers to write together. That way they'd end up with a whole song instead of half a song. It was good business for them, and an invaluable training ground for a new writer who hadn't yet developed his or her own contacts within the industry.

EMI put me with all these great black writers, and they even sent me to Nashville to work with Tony Joe White. I had met Tony Joe at a party thrown by his Australian manager, Roger Davies. Roger played him my 'So Lucky' album and he asked to meet me. If ever there was a man capable of reducing a cynical girl to a ball of mush, this was him. Extraordinarily handsome in a rugged kind of way, he looks like a better version of Kris Kristofferson – unassuming and seemingly unaware of his effect on women, making him even more devastating. He was very much married, and happily so, I was told, so I soon let thoughts of a dalliance drift away.

What was really great about my meeting Tony Joe White was the fact that, on hearing me sing, he had wanted to write with me. Looking back, I'm amazed at his intuitiveness in seeing the potential in me that only Pat Lucas had seen before. I was scared but thrilled, and my publishers arranged my trip to Nashville immediately.

So there I was, on a plane to Nashville, wondering what the fuck I was doing trying to write with the great Tony Joe

White. When I got to his house he took me down to the basement where he had a little pignose amp, a mouth organ and a drum machine set up. He played around with different chords, and I just starting singing melodies, hoping something would click. When I was on the right track, his eyes lit up and it sent him off into another chord-searching frenzy. That's how we spent most of the day, amid the odd tobacco-chewing and spitting bout. (Him, not me!)

At the end of each session (we worked for two days) he would tell me to go on up to the porch where his wife and mother would have cold lemonade waiting for me. Our conversations were kind of like Ma and Pa Kettle in rocking chairs. *How y'all laak it here in Nashville? It's a kind a drah heat here, init? Ah hear Australia has a kinda drah heat too … Uhuh … A'd love to go down there some day.*

Meanwhile, Tony Joe would emerge from the basement with an Esky and bid us bye-bye before disappearing into the bushes across the road. His wife said she didn't know what he did behind those bushes, but every day at four o'clock, off he'd go. (Methinks Tony Joe was up to no good in them there bushes.)

By the way, the song we eventually wrote together was 'Gonna Take a Long Time', a pretty ordinary ditty that went nowhere. But what a great experience!

The EMI songwriting deal kept my rent paid for the rest of my stay in the US. I really earned it, though: it was no mean feat having to come up with fifteen songs every year to comply with the contract. In the meantime, I was still doing all kinds of singing jobs in between.

One of the jobs I got was with the Mojo advertising agency in Australia. They had an account for a new Swan lager beer aimed at women and they were going to do this big ad campaign. Someone played the agency 'It's a Man's Man's World' from my 'Basement Live' album, and Mojo decided that that should be the song to promote this new 'women's beer'. They flew to America to re-record it with me, and then flew me back first class to shoot the commercial. The beer didn't sell. I think they underestimated the women of Australia in the patronising way they addressed them, attempting to use feminism to draw them to the product. A good beer is a good beer, and apparently this wasn't.

Michael Lang negotiated $A50 000 for me to do the ad. I was in a euphoric daze spending that money. Faster than a speeding bullet I bought myself clothes, Art Deco furniture and a secondhand Mercedes. I took my friends out to celebrate. I remember disposing of that money in world-record time.

Two weeks later the car died on me: the whole suspension fell out of it and it was irreparable. I had been royally ripped off … it was God's message. Not that it changed me in any way. Because I was broke so often, when I got a lot of money I would just explode, thinking that there was always more where that came from. I'm always in awe of people who hoard money and have heaps they know they can spend if they want to, but don't. I've always wondered what that would be like. It must be the equivalent of being about to have an orgasm and holding it back.

My disaster with the Mercedes marked the beginning of my period of renting cars from Rent-A-Wreck. This company had great old Mustang convertibles and Thunderbirds, so for the next four or five years I rented the sorts of cars I would have loved to buy but couldn't afford. The good thing was, if the car broke down, their motto was, 'just leave it there, call us, and we'll just bring you another one.' The cars broke down a lot.

I made some wonderful friends during my time in LA. There was Johnny Lee Schell and his wife Beth, my buddy Terry Becker, and another great sound engineer, Lenise Bent. There was also Connie, my friend who used to work as an assistant to Jack Nicholson and Phil Spector amongst others. Then there was Andre Fisher who played drums with Rufus and ended up marrying Natalie Cole, and Steve Harvey, my mad Scottish friend, who is the blackest white man (musically) that I have ever met. All these people sustained me during the hard times.

I remember once, on my thirty-fourth birthday in 1987, another good friend, Mark Leonard (the bass player in the movie *The Rose* with Bette Midler), took me out for a surprise night. The early part of the day had been a bit bumpy, however. I'd been rehearsing with Easy Pieces when a policeman had come into the rehearsal room talking about a stolen Mercedes in the carpark, and asking who was the owner of that car. (This was before the car died on me.) Everybody stared at me, and I started to sweat. *Oh my God, could this really be happening to me? Have I just bought a stolen car?* Somewhere in the back of my mind I smelt a rat, 'cause this cop had immaculately plucked eyebrows and just a hint of gloss on his lips. Even with these warning signs that this might not have been entirely kosher, I was still in a panic. In the midst of this, from somewhere came disco music (mmm, my favourite). The policeman was a male stripper. To my horror, he gyrated and then straddled me where I sat, while the whole band, including one of the wives who had organised this, looked on with glee.

Thank goodness the best of my birthday was yet to come.

After a nice shower and a fresh face I was picked up by Mark, who drove me to the MTV music awards where Prince, who was my favourite artist at the time, was performing. Then we had an incredible dinner at a Japanese restaurant (I was a saki expert by now). Finally, Mark blindfolded me and we drove to an undisclosed location where, after leading me in through the door, he removed my blindfold to reveal that I was in the Country Club in downtown LA, where performers did private showcases for their record companies. We sat down at a table right at the front. I couldn't for the life of me guess who the performer would be, or who Mark Leonard would think he could impress me with.

As the lights went down and the curtain went up, I got shivers up my back. There on stage was 'Kat', the main dancer for Prince, setting up the mood for one of the best concerts of my life. Prince did this one impromptu private show while he was in LA after the awards, and I was there. He played for about three and a half hours. Normally I can't sit in a chair for half an hour without wanting to get up and leave, but this was gripping stuff. Prince tends to be a little 'androidish' at his shows, but on this night it was total spontaneity between him and his band. I will always love my friend Mark for organising that night for me.

When I did the occasional show, I had a fantastic band – Andre Fisher (from the old Rufus) on drums, Don Griffith (also from Rufus) on guitar, Freddie Washington on bass, and singer Penny Ford on background vocals. Penny was also one of Chaka Khan's background singers. At my rehearsals she was always saying, 'You gotta meet Chaka, you gotta meet Chaka.'

Yeah, yeah, yeah. Eventually Penny played the 'Easy Pieces' album to her and Chaka fell in love with one of the tracks I co-wrote, 'You're My Heaven'. She told Penny to tell me so.

It turned out that Chaka had to do these two dates in Carolina and one of the girls in her background group (the low-voiced one) was not able to do it, so Penny thought of me. She didn't know whether I would do it or not, because to her I was always a solo singer, so when she asked me she wasn't sure how I would take it. *Would I do background vocals for Chaka Khan?! Are you kidding?* Ego never came into it. I've always learned so much from situations like this. I jumped at it.

Chaka can't work without singers. The intricate three- or four-part harmonies she does, backing herself, are part of the trademark of her records. It also means that any background singers she uses almost certainly have to sound like her. Anyone who comes to Chaka is a fan and sounds like her anyway. That was the first thing that struck me when I got to meet the background girls. Also, the girls were tiny in height, but really well-built, again like Chaka. Beside them I must have seemed like a huge, clumsy white blob.

Because most female singers in America know all her songs, Chaka assumed that I wasn't going to need rehearsals. She was quite surprised that I wasn't that familiar with all her material. 'Who have you been listening to?' *Aretha!* She liked that. She also liked the fact that I was different from everyone else, from the way I spoke to my sense of humour. Also, we were the same age. We both grew up on the same kinds of music and had had similar careers, though on opposite sides of the world. We hit it off.

I learned Chaka's material in world-record time with Penny Ford as my coach.

We had to get off in North Carolina and change planes for South Carolina where the first gig was. Chaka had just got her period and she asked me to go around the terminal to find some tampons. Finally I returned to the Ladies room to find Chaka and Penny in a cubicle together. 'Come on in, wild Aussie girl!' So there I was, freebasing cocaine with Penny while Chaka was organising her tampon.

Chaka and I are similar in a lot of ways. We're both mischievous and a bit cynical. For an American musician to be that way is rare, though, and I think she was glad to share that side of herself with someone. She's a great singer. I have huge respect for her. She sings imaginatively all the time and she has incredible pitch and phrasing. It's no surprise she's regarded as one of the all-time greatest soul singers. (After Aretha, that is.)

In South Carolina, Chaka kept the audience waiting for three hours. Eventually she got there, and though the crowd was angry, she sang her heart out for them and all was forgiven. But the promoter was furious. He and Chaka's manager had a fight and the next morning we were told we were all going back to LA.

Eventually Chaka and her band went on tour to Japan. They asked me to go with them, but I decided not to. Chaka and I were a dangerous combination.

John McLain was still doing his bit for me, always trying to hook me up with people. He was determined to show off this great talent he'd found.

I gotta give it to him, he really did try. One night he took me to dinner and afterwards suggested we drop in on Sting's recording session. As part of the 'Nothing Like the Sun' album, Sting wanted to record one track produced by the black department at A&M. John oversaw it and got an up-and-coming producer called Brian Loren to produce it. The track was 'We'll Be Together'. John and I dropped into Larrabe Studios (in Hollywood) after our meal to hear the track they were about to mix. After listening to what had been done, John said, 'Those background singers ain't shit. They got no power. You gotta get Renée on this.' So they had me and Vesta Williams, a big-voiced black girl who was also signed to A&M at the time, re-do the whole thing till four o'clock in the morning. Sting was there at the beginning, but after a while it became clear that he could trust us, so he left it in our hands and went wandering off into the night.

During the recording session the uncool Australian struck again. There I was with Vesta, singing my heart out. It sounded incredible. Vesta turned to me at one point and said, 'Man, you stink!' I've since learned that this is a compliment when your singing or playing sounds real down and dirty. But at the time I just stood there, frozen, thinking, *It must be my BO* (it had been a long session, after all). Everybody had a bit of a laugh and I joined in with a fake one.

Most of the end of the 'We'll Be Together' track is me wailing. They kept it all. The backgrounds that Vesta and I created on that song are the most powerful I've ever heard. John made sure I got paid some big bucks for that one. They spelt my name wrong on the album, but I got so much more work out of it, it didn't matter. That song was a big hit around the world, and at the time, everybody wanted that vocal sound.

Another job that came through A&M was singing backgrounds on Toni Childs' album, 'Union'. Toni seemed insecure about her beautiful but very unusual voice. I had no idea her album was going to be the huge hit that it was, and I suspect she didn't either.

Cuban arranger/producer Umberto Gattica used me on many things. I did a lot of layering of my voice for him. If he had a small budget he could rely on me to create a whole choir for him. I loved working with him, especially when it was a Cuban project ... and there were quite a few of those. Umberto has become very successful and recently produced the duet with Celine Dion and Barbra Streisand.

I worked with many people in the three years after the Sting song.

I mainly remember the producers, not so much the acts. It was always unusual work because word got around that I could do a few different sounds. Also, being uninhibited, I got the reputation for being willing to try anything to make a track work. They knew that if they were stuck for a melody in a song, I usually came up with something.

David Foster got me for a couple of sessions where I had to be completely disciplined and clear-voiced for 'oohs' and 'ahhs' – my least favourite thing to do – although I got to wail a little bit at the end of a Neil Diamond track that he produced. I remember Foster being charming but very anal in his approach to making records. Everything had to be perfect, and that usually meant singing the part over and over again to the point of distraction. You can hear this over-produced style on most of his records with people like The Corrs, Celine Dion, Whitney Houston and Barbra Streisand. Very slick and a little soulless.

Through the English blues producer John Porter I sang on Buddy Guy's 'Feels Like Rain' album. Buddy was charming, an absolute gentleman. I sang backing vocals on his version of Marvin Gaye's 'Some Kind of Wonderful', which Paul Rodgers sang on, and I did a duet with Bonnie Raitt on the title track, a John Hiatt song. John Porter and I got on great. He was someone who was genuinely interested in making a record with me, but we just never found the time. The other thing is, I didn't want to make a blues record, which was his forte.

Through John I also got to do a gig at the Roxy (the legendary night spot in Hollywood) with Taj Mahal. It was for Taj's record launch. He'd recently done a duet of the song 'Mockingbird' with Etta James on his new record. When she couldn't make the launch, they asked me to fill in for her. It could have been an incredible night, but I had a migraine. I can't explain in words how painful it is to try and sing with one of these. I managed to do my number and gave it all I had. It went down well, but I couldn't bask in any glory or just hang out with these people after the gig. My head was throbbing so I split immediately after the song. I was waiting next door, in the famous 'Rainbow Club' carpark, to be picked up, and I looked up and there was Ringo Starr having a cigarette in the parking lot. 'Are you the girl that was just on stage?' he asked. 'You're great … Are you going back in to sing some more?'

I'd finally met my first Beatle and all I wanted to do was ask if he had any painkillers.

Jackson Browne is a bit of a walking contradiction. His songs are sad and a bit dark, and when I first heard his music and learned about his first wife committing suicide, I attached all this mystique to him. When I finally met him, he wasn't a mysterious type at all, just a very normal kind of Californian guy. Bonnie Raitt introduced Jackson to my music and he used to turn up at whatever gig I was doing in LA. At one point he was producing an album for John Trudell, the native-American poet/activist. I sang on a track and did a harmony with Kris Kristofferson. He'd already done his part, so I had to shadow it, with Jackson instructing.

Jackson Brown has got an Australian son, and unbeknownst to me he was over here holidaying with him on the Gold Coast when I was appearing at the Byron Bay Blues Festival in 1995. He must have seen the ads, because he came to see me. At the end of the show, there was Jackson Browne's hand reaching up to help me get down from the stage. All these press people suddenly swarmed around me and Jackson – it was bizarre: 'the Blues paparazzi'! Unfortunately they didn't get much action – Jackson was here on holidays and not doing any press. I remember my band really liking him, and vice versa. We had a great afternoon with him and, at the end, in the pouring rain, he helped push our bogged van out of the mud. (I eventually sang on his 'Looking East' album on one of my later visits back to LA.)

Every year I get Christmas cookies from Jackson and he stays in touch.

By 1991 I was immersed in writing songs with all sorts of people, while still doing everything possible to get my own recording career going. That's when Paul Kelly came into my life in a major way and turned things around.

I first met Paul back in the early eighties when we were Mushroom labelmates. We'd pass each other in the corridors. Certain songs of his always struck me. Back then he was dark, with unmanageable hair, incredibly black eyes and a single eyebrow. I always thought he was intense and mysterious.

In late 1991 I was invited back to Sydney to appear on the Martin Armiger-produced soundtrack for the ABC's 'Seven Deadly Sins' series. Paul was also involved, as was Vika Bull and Deborah Conway. One of the songs submitted was 'Foggy Highway', written by Paul. I don't think it was originally intended for me to sing, but somehow I reluctantly had a bash at it late one night at Martin's request. It's not that I didn't like the song, it was just a kind of simple, sparse and spooky melody and lyric that I wasn't sure was my cup of tea. It was very late; a soulful time of night, and I sang it in one take. From the moment I did, that song became mine. Martin thought it was quite beautiful, and I agreed, it sounded pretty good.

I went back to America, and a few weeks later there was a message on my machine from Paul Kelly saying how moved he was by my rendition. He said it was the best that anyone else had ever sung one of his songs. I called him back to thank him for the compliment and found out that he was travelling back and forth to America, so I suggested that he look me up and we pursue something – maybe a co-writing thing, or maybe he had something else for me to sing? All I knew is that I wanted to do more with this incredibly talented guy, and that he saw something in me that I'd overlooked. After all the ego battering of America, I'd forgotten that my gift was to simply sing songs from my heart.

'Foggy Highway' marked the beginning of a new approach to finding great songs.

Paul and his wife, Kaarin Fairfax, and their firstborn little girl, Madeleine, came over to my house in Lauren Canyon and our friendship grew from there. They stayed at the Highland Apartments in Hollywood and I'd visit them often, usually to co-write or just to hear what Paul was working on. By now I was becoming a huge fan of his. Everything he worked on seemed so etched in the earth, so heartfelt. To this day I rarely dislike anything he comes up with. It might not sometimes be something I'd pick for myself, but it's always extremely soulful. Paul became a really good friend and an objective adviser in my musical life.

Around this time I asked Paul if he'd write a song especially for me. He came up with 'Difficult Woman'. It was a beautiful description of a strong, misunderstood, complicated but vulnerable girl, and, although the title unnerved me for a minute, I was knocked out by the song.

He suggested I make another album. It just sort of happened. I think I said, *Well, if you produce it I'll make it.* Paul asked Australian film producer Bob Weiss if he would finance it, and Bob kindly came up with the money. We used a lot of my contacts – people who owed me favours, musicians and studios, and we hired Terry Becker, my old friend from the 'So Lucky' days, as engineer.

I decided to re-do a few of Paul's older songs. We turned 'Sweet Guy' into a waltz (it had had more of a rock'n'roll feel before). We also did 'Careless' with an 'Everybody's Talkin'' kind of feel. Paul and I were both very much into Brazilian music at the time. We co-wrote 'Summer, Winter, Spring and Fall' and we invited this Brazilian guitarist/singer, Dory Caymmi, to perform on the song. He played the six-string guitar beautifully, and hummed. That was his style. After his one take, he came out to listen and he said, 'I sound like a drunk priest,' which was great because he *looked* like a drunk priest. To me that's one of my favourite tracks on any of my records.

It was around this time and through EMI that I struck up a friendship and working relationship with John Clifforth. He was in the Australian band Deck Chairs Overboard in the early eighties and, like me, went to New York and then LA and eventually became a writer for EMI. He and I wrote some songs for 'Difficult Woman' as well.

The album was a joy to make. It was quite sparse, darkish and unadorned, and I sang in a softer, huskier voice than usual. It's through that record that I developed a sweeter sound to my voice. People who had never heard of me before loved this record, but some people who loved me as a belter were a little uncomfortable with it. Overall, though, it's a record that's won a lot of critical acclaim.

Some American labels were initially interested in the record, but the deals just never came through. They loved the sound of my voice but they didn't know how to market me. (Here we go again ...) So we started pitching the album to Australia. Michael Gudinski rang me in LA and said, 'Look, Renée, I can't hear any hits on this record but the staff love it so I'll give you a little deal.'

I didn't want a little deal. I said thanks but no thanks and went to Larrikin Records, who also offered me a little deal but with really high hopes and they loved the record to death. Michael never quite forgave me for that.

Larrikin was really into the record, but what I didn't know was that poor Larrikin had no clout. They couldn't even get me on the TV shows that I could normally get myself. Their policy was that if they sold 5000 copies they were happy, so they never budgeted for anything bigger than that, marketing-wise. I had such hopes for that record. Although my audiences connect 'Difficult Woman' (the song) with me, sadly I don't think as many people know about the album.

I had a lot of fantastic musical experiences in America, but they were too few and far between. They couldn't sustain me financially, and I didn't feel fulfilled.

It took a good ol' boy from Australia (Paul Kelly) to remind me that I was really talented.

Through his faith in me and the beautiful record we made together, I slowly got my confidence back.

I was starting to get homesick for Australia.

The LA earthquake in early 1994 seemed like a bit of a sign ... maybe I should go home. This earthquake freaked me out more than any other I had experienced before. Even the tough LA cynics who usually laughed at people's hysterical reactions were strangely silent after this one. It was huge. At four o'clock in the morning, sometime in late January, it was as if a giant picked up a box, which was my apartment, and shook it violently for thirty seconds – an eternity. With the apartment shaking non-stop, I managed to climb out of bed and hold onto the post. All I could think of at this time when I felt sure I was going to die was, firstly, where's my bra? I didn't want to be carried out topless – and, secondly, how am I going to die? Are the walls going to cave in? Is the roof going to fall down? Or do I simply go through the floor? I had never been so interested in the construction of a building in my entire life. I just stood there, waiting to die, listening to glass shattering and things falling, and thinking that the town had been levelled.

Then, just as suddenly as it started, it stopped. Dead silence. No power: just darkness. And then the faint, distant sound of sirens, gradually getting louder and louder. After getting help from a neighbour who had a torch, I surveyed the damage. Everything in my apartment that wasn't in the dishwasher was shattered. In the midst of the rubble, it hit me: *Where's Mr Big, my cat?* We went on a panicked search of the apartment and finally found him, wedged behind the toilet. It took us a quarter of an hour to get him out of there. He was in shock.

Within one week I was out of LA. Mr Big and I secured ourselves a New York apartment that I organised over the phone with my credit card at lightening speed. As if the quake wasn't enough, I returned to New York at a time when the city was experiencing one of the worst snowstorms it had had in many years.

Another sign.

So here I was, back in New York. I'd come full circle. I was doing demos again (although I was also writing some of them as well, now), sliding twelve blocks in the snow because I couldn't afford a cab, doing a fifty-dollar demo, and sliding back or grabbing a cab with the money I had just made.

By now the novelty of struggling in America was wearing thin. The only bright sparks for me were the odd job, and calling my friends in LA and Australia who I was starting to miss terribly. But New York was a great distraction for me at a low time.

In the six months I was there I started seriously thinking of returning to Australia.

The main thing stopping me was my cat, Mr Big. I was very attached to him, and because he was an older cat I didn't want him to go through the three to six months quarantine he'd have been subjected to if I brought him into this country.

That was keeping me in America. I was literally not going to leave because of my pussycat.

In the last two months before I left, Mr Big became terminally ill with feline leukaemia. That levelled me. I tried everything I could to cure him, going to all the vet specialists in New York, but in the end he had to be put down. No more Mr Big to worry about … I was heartsick.

I felt like Mr Big died to let me go home.

I wasn't planning to come home for good. I was just going to return for a while and see what unfolded, but the longer I stayed, the more I decided that it was just as easy for me to be based here and go back to the US, rather than the other way around. There was more for me to do in Australia. Besides, the world had become so much smaller. You didn't have to be based in a place where you wanted to release records. You could do it from anywhere.

It's been six years since I left America, and I have to say, as much as I love my life here in Australia, whenever anyone asks me if I'm here to stay, it's still very much a case of, *America, I ain't finished with you yet!*

Chapter 11

SEX

I've loved many people, but I don't think I've ever been in love.

Up until I was about sixteen years of age, all my sexual experiences were in my little room, in my little head. I never had experiences as dangerous and exciting in real life as I did in my dreams.

My mum bought me my first record, 'Normie Rowe A Go Go', when I was nine. I thought he was so sexy. I even loved it when he got charged with carnal knowledge with a twelve-year-old girl. I thought, *How fantastic! It could be me.* Everyone was shocked and horrified by Normie's behaviour, but it just made me love him even more. His music wasn't why I wanted his record: it was just the thought of Normie grunting away. He was very animalistic-looking in those days.

Me and the girl who lived next door would pretend we had boyfriends. We imagined them on the walls of our bedrooms and we kissed them passionately. My idol was the TV star James Drury, better known as The Virginian. He was dark and brooding. This kind of man became the source of my most elaborate fantasies. I used to sit in my room and put sweaters on my head, pretending that I had long hair, and there I'd be, making love to James Drury against the wall.

At the end of my street lived the Coronius brothers. Their house backed onto a lane which I had to walk down in order to catch the train to and from school. On the other side of the hostel, across the main road, was a home for wayward girls. On my way home, one or both of the brothers would always be with one or other of those girls in that laneway, and I would have to wait till their trysts were over before I could pass by. I got quite an education watching them in that laneway. There was a lot of necking, hitching of dresses and pulling down of undies – much too much for a girl of my age to be seeing, but incredible fodder for my dreams at night. Alone in my room I was wanton, loose, adventurous – all the things I never was in real life.

The Coronius brothers were never in my dreams, though. I had crushes on people like Alain Delon. I especially loved him in that movie *Borsalino*. My girlfriends at the time loved Jean Paul Belmondo, his partner. I couldn't believe it: how could they prefer the boxer-nosed mealy-mouthed Belmondo to such an Adonis as Delon? I also loved George Harrison, Tyrone Power and Dana Andrews. I remember seeing Humphrey Bogart with Lauren Bacall in *To Have and Have Not*, and I could feel his mouth when she kissed him. I could really taste it. I was so in love with Humphrey Bogart. I also loved Elvis, until his corset period.

When I lived at home I was only allowed out every second weekend, and even then I had to be back home three or four hours later. There wasn't a whole lot a girl could get up to in that short length of time.

My early social life consisted of dances every second weekend, Jewish social clubs and going to the beach — a *lot* of going down to Bondi Beach. I loved summer. I loved waking up in the holidays, smelling a hot day and then going down to the beach. I'd be in the water until I got crinkly and shivery. I loved watching the surfers from South Bondi, but I mainly hung out with my Jewish friends on the steps in the middle of the beach. That spot was known as 'little Jerusalem'. Every year there'd be a new fashion in swimsuits and my mother would take me to Grace Brothers in Bondi Junction and buy me a new bikini. I used to stuff the bras. My breasts only emerged when I was about sixteen.

My parents tried as hard as they could to corral me into the Jewish social scene, but I was always on the fringe, standing in front of the band at the dances with all the non-Jews. I remember at one of those dances sitting down in between songs when some boy came up to me and asked, 'Would you like to dance?' *Yes, please.* As I got up, towering over him, he took one look, said, 'Never mind,' and walked away. I'll never forget that.

I was a bean shoot; I had no figure. I was very skinny and very tall, freckly and blue-eyed — very non-Jewish looking. I used to feel quite ugly amongst the juicy plump Jewish girls in my youth group, but my mother used to say, 'Don't you worry. Wait till you get older. You watch; you'll get all the action.' She was right. I had much more luck later in life. I noticed that most of those lusty, busty, big-arsed girls who were popular with the boys back then became matronly way before their time.

I got my first period when my mother and father were overseas. I was fifteen and Mrs Goodsell, my mother's friend and helper at the hostel, a few years before, was minding us. I'd been feeling strange all day, with this ache in my lower tummy that I'd never felt before. But when I went to the toilet that night I knew. Mrs Goodsell handled it very coolly and calmly. She made me a nice plate of potato pancakes and chatted to me about what it all signified. I knew, anyway. By that time they were already preparing girls for 'becoming a woman' at school.

I only ever had one crush on a *real* guy when I was little. I first met him when my parents catered for his Bar Mitzvah. At thirteen years of age, he was two years older than me. He was dark, handsome, quiet, brooding and very smart. In later years we'd see each other at dances at the Great Synagogue or the Temple Emanuel, and of course at the beach. We'd go down to the steps of Bondi Beach for most of the day, then at about three in the afternoon we'd pile into someone's fancy car and drive up to Camp Cove, past Watson's Bay. Camp Cove was a chic little beach, and everyone went there to show off – bikinis, boyfriends or girlfriends, cars ... It was a little flirting paradise. Whilst this boy and I had some pretty passionate make-out sessions, we never consummated the relationship. All through my secondary school years, however, he was The One. I ran into him years later and discovered that he'd had a major thing for me too. If only I'd known. I never thought he liked me as much as I liked him, so I'd always acted cool and stand-offish, not wanting him to know.

This became an unfortunate pattern throughout my life.

I started singing with bands straight after leaving school, and as a consequence I never really had any dates. You didn't date musicians back in the seventies, you just hung out with them. When we weren't working we were happy to be in each others' company at a club or someone's house, just hanging out. In those early days, on our nights off, we would often go down to Chequers in Goulburn Street, Sydney. This was after it had been turned from a theatre-cabaret room into a discotheque, with young bands playing there. That's where most musicians and roadies would go for a drink after their own gigs.

I'd start getting dressed to go out at ten o'clock at night, when most people were winding down and getting ready for bed. I would wear tight jeans and get incredibly made-up to look as sexy as possible. At the age of seventeen or eighteen, most girls go out in groups. I never really did that. Because I hung out with musicians and was regarded as one of them, I had the courage to go out alone, and it never looked like I was going out to get boys. But in actual fact I had a bit of an agenda – flirting – and I was dressed to kill for it.

When you went to these clubs during the day for rehearsal, they were graveyards of ash and they smelt of stale bourbon. But at night-time they were delicious and glamorous, always promising the chance for some incredibly romantic adventure to take place.

I was starting to discover the power of my body. No longer was I the gangly creature of my Jewish youth group days. As my mother had predicted, I'd grown into a buxom beauty. This was the hippy era and I never used to wear a bra. One of the places I visited on my nights off was the Arts Factory, a famous venue for up-and-coming bands. I remember walking through the doors one night, past Michael Chugg, who is now a famous promoter of live entertainment. Back then he managed the New Zealand band the La De Das. As I walked past, Chuggy went, 'They're the biggest tits I've ever seen.' I've never *not* worn a bra since.

Guys seemed to lust after me. It was a double bunger: 'Not only can she sing like that, but she looks good too!' I was young, full-lipped, natural and apparently had no inhibitions (if only they knew ...). I had this 'go anywhere, do anything' air about me. I always acted confident, but in truth I never was. It was just a front so as not to let anyone know how scared I was underneath.

Every time I went out it was a performance ... at the bar looking good, ordering the drink (always scotch and soda, no ice), flirting a little bit, then off to the Ladies room to fix the make-up and come back out for another scene in the play. I never got drunk, but I drank a lot. I could drink most people under the table, and drinking always made me feel sexy. I would spot someone interesting, hone in on him and usually spend the rest of the evening with him, talking and drinking for hours amid hugging and kissing. After more necking during the ride home, finally there was always the inevitable tussle in the car at the end of the ride because I just wanted to go to bed, alone. For a long time I never went further than that with anyone.

Sometimes I was called a prick teaser, and in a way I guess I was. I never intentionally played havoc with these boys, though. For me it was like Clayton's sex: the sex you have when you're not having sex; sex without the problems. It was enough for me at the time to know that I could get men excited but not have to commit to anything or anyone, thereby eliminating any chance of rejection. Oh, I had lusts and dreams, for sure, but I could never quite let go.

I already had a broad imagination and I'd seen lots of things. Nothing shocked me. When I was eighteen I went on a tour of Asia, singing for the Australian troops (care of the ABC). After one of our shows in Thailand, a group of soldiers took me and some of the others to see the 'Egg Lady of Penang'. She did amazing feats with her vagina and I wasn't shocked one bit. Fascinated, but not shocked. In fact, I even thought how rude it was of the audience not to applaud after each of her tricks. This lady could hold an egg inside her vagina and lay it whenever she wanted to. She could fill up a family-sized Coca-Cola bottle with water, put the water up inside her, and then, when she wanted to, let it out. At the end of her show she crouched and painted, with a brush inserted in her vagina, the words 'The End' onto a sheet of paper for an audience member to take home as a souvenir.

In the very early seventies I gave the impression that I was fucking everybody. I guess I didn't want anyone to know that I wasn't. But the truth was that I just didn't want to do it yet. Every time I went out with somebody I held out hopes that this might be the guy who would make me want to make love. I even remember having discussions with Mother Earth's drummer about it, saying, *I don't know when I'm going to do this. I'm so scared.* He was like, 'I understand. Let me help you.' I declined his kind offer.

When eventually I lost my virginity, I was twenty. It was some time in early 1973 and I was doing a residency at this club in Sydney called the Rocks Push. All sorts of notable musicians would drop by after their gigs (our shows went very late). One guy in particular caught my eye. He was dark, kinda shy and brooding ... just my type. I'd seen him before – he was a friend of the boys in the band. He was also a great singer. For months we flirted with each other and talked of our mutual vocal inspirations (we both adored Donny Hathaway). I put on my best 'been there, seen it all' act.

Then one night as he drove me home, we parked and started making out pretty heavily.

He asked, could we go to his friend's place where he was staying at the time? I decided to go for it: now or never.

I really thought this was going to be *it* until we got into the bedroom. He went straight for the sixty-nine position. I was in shock. *What? No foreplay?* I was lying there, facing this ... view, and he was at the opposite end, facing his view. Sure, we *were* both hot and passionate before this point, but I'd hoped we might *ease* into the act of making love. My tough front had worked to my detriment: he thought I was waiting for this.

Finally I got up the courage up to say, *Stop!* He was shocked. 'What? What?' I said, *I'm sorry to have to tell you this, but I'm a virgin and this is just a little fast for me, so we won't be doing this right now. Goodbye.* I got dressed, went outside, hailed a cab and went home, leaving this poor man shell-shocked.

Ironically, this was the man who I later ended up making love with for the first time. He persevered with me for three or four months after that night. I'd thought he would drop me like a hotcake, discovering that I was a fraud, but he found it endearing and, I guess, special because I'd been honest with him. He liked the fact that this girl, who everyone thought of as worldly, was his secret little virgin. He wooed me, won my trust and became my first boyfriend.

I got pregnant with that first guy. Twice.

I'd been living away from home already for three years, so I wasn't afraid to tell my mother. Straightaway she took me to a Hungarian doctor's private home on Sydney's North Shore. Abortions were illegal in those days and quite hard to get, especially if you didn't want a backyard operation. I remember just wanting to get it over with. I was much too young to think about the seriousness of it all. My mother knew me so well. What would I have done with a baby? I was so unreliable and rebellious; I wasn't ready for motherhood.

My boyfriend totally agreed.

While the doctor was getting on with the procedure I stared at a picture on the wall showing what was happening to the foetus, what they were actually doing to this baby in my womb. It was a horrible picture that I'll never forget, put there I'm sure to teach girls like me a lesson. The operation was very clean and very organised, but cold and uncompassionate. I was being made to feel that I was a very bad girl.

I inherited fertility from my mother. She knew how easy it could happen, so with her, abortion wasn't a moral issue. She just wanted to help me. I am one of the only people I know who got pregnant on the pill. Out of six pregnancies, three of them happened while I was taking some form of contraception. I know that abortion is a tricky issue for a lot of people. I'm not a person who rejoices in the fact that I've had to terminate these pregnancies, but the alternative – bringing a child into the world to be brought up by someone with no sense of responsibility – always left me with no choice. I think, in the end, I did the right thing, but I was always sad and very depressed after each procedure.

It was directly after I split up with my first boyfriend that I realised I was pregnant to him for the second time. Despite the fact that he was eleven years older than me, his insecurities were greater than mine. He always used to say, 'Now that you've been with me, I know you'll leave me as soon as you find someone else.' I used to tell him he was being silly. He was right.

We'd been together for about a year when he developed a hernia. During his hospital stay, I somehow lost my feeling for him. He was married with kids. (Did I forget to mention this?) He never had any intention of leaving his wife for me. Somehow, it hadn't worried me until now. I'd been living a pretty busy musical and social life, so I never questioned the fact that we only spent two or three nights a week together. But when I ran into the wife and kids at the hospital, everything was brought home to me. I had to admit, it was time to move on. By the time I realised I was pregnant to him again, I was already in Melbourne doing the 'It's a Man's Man's World' album. I remember a lot of phone calls back and forth about the abortion, this time him asking, 'Are you sure? Are you sure?' I was sure.

Melbourne was the start of my new life, musically as well as sexually. After making 'It's a Man's Man's World' I fell madly for the sound guy of our touring band. I was always attracted to the sound and lighting crew. I liked their humour and their uncomplicatedness, the way they just got things done with ease. I also liked the way they looked when they did what they did.

I really pursued this guy. He was very shy and there were many girls on the road who fancied him. There were cat and mouse games all the time and I pretended I didn't care for him at first, but I did – I really wanted him. I reeled him in, I played him, and I got him.

I was twenty-two when he and I moved into our own little rented house in Brighton, Melbourne. We lasted together for about four or five years, moving to Sydney during that time and then back to Melbourne again. He was the only person I've ever lived with romantically. It was a happy experience, for the most part, except for a few little incidents. He had a dark streak, which led to a few scary moments where I feared for my safety.

We were arguing a lot. Dabbling in heroin didn't help either. In 1978, after hopes for keeping it together were dashed with constant fights about drugs and petty, jealous rages, our relationship ended.

I remember most of the guys I was with – even the one-nighters. I was with several men in the seventies and the eighties and I had some of the best times of my life. By now, I loved sex, and the wilder times I had were due in part to one little pill called Mandrax.

Today's generation may not be familiar with this pill. It was a sleeping aid that did *anything* but make you want to go to sleep. Anyone who had any sort of a sexual hang-up loosened up quick when they took Mandrax. I was still picky about who I wanted to be with, but the inhibitions were gone.

There was one time in early 1975 when a whole bunch of famous rock'n'roll stars of the day assembled in a hotel room in Melbourne, smoking joints and passing around a bottle of Mandrax. Me and one of the guys started making eye contact. (That was always the exciting part – the eye contact, the secret signs ... Message understood.) This guy was someone who everybody, including me, had lusted after for a long time. After what seemed like endless minutes of eye contact, *phhhtt!* off to his room we went. Apparently he shared this room with another member of his band, who must have been making eye contact of his own with some other girl, because halfway through the night I became aware of the fact that we weren't alone. There was me and this guy, plus his roommate and his girlfriend, going at it hammer and tongs ... Not a foursome; just two couples oblivious to anything else but each other. At some point I (who normally gets embarrassed by even a shop assistant seeing me in my undies) remember looking up for a second and thinking, *This is debauchery ... This is mad!* Mandrax – no inhibitions.

The next day I had to be at a soundcheck for a show I was performing at the Dallas Brooks Hall that night. I left a note on the pillow while my guy was asleep, saying, *Thanks, it was beautiful. See you later, I hope.* I loved being able to walk out of his room and wait to see if he'd turn up that night at my gig. He did ... like the bee to the honey.

On another occasion around this time, I remember being in my room with this same guy in the house I shared with Michael Gudinski and Ray Evans in Toorak. It was after one of the Mushroom parties. I remember looking up in the middle of love-making to see singer Leo DeCastro's face looking down at us through the little window above my door, smiling that truly mad smile he had. Leo was an amazing Maori soul singer – one of the best ever in this country – but he was a wild man. Nuts. He must have moseyed up the stairs after the party, looking for action. He'd probably heard sounds coming out of the bedroom, so he got himself a chair, climbed up on it, and just watched the whole thing. We shoo'd him away, had a giggle, and carried on as if nothing happened. Mandrax strikes again.

What I liked about this lover, and consequently most of the guys I've ended up falling for, was his absolute unabashed love of a woman and her body. Guys like this loved in an almost animalistic, can't-get-enough way. You were on a complete ride to heaven with them. This kind of man was incredibly confident and at ease with his hands, his mouth and his body ... *and* he was usually funny too. You felt like the most wanted woman in the world. That's sexy.

Over the years I've had people come up to me and say, 'I know you fucked So-and-so', or a band member will say, 'So-and-so told someone you had to fuck all the musicians before they could be in your band'. These kinds of comments have always astounded me. I mean, remember Nut Man? Remember Mean Man? There were some guys I was definitely *not* going to touch.

I've very rarely been with anyone from one of my bands. At least, not while we were *in* a band together. For me and the guys in the band it was always about the music. The one exception I made to this rule was with the drummer from my 'Ready To Deal' band in late 1975. It was an extraordinary situation in extraordinary times. He was the first black American I'd ever encountered close up, and I couldn't help but fall for him. He was irresistible.

We'd made the record together, mixed it and mastered it, but nothing happened until the launch of the 'Ready To Deal' album in Sydney. We all got very drunk that night, and he and I just zeroed in on each other. At an after-launch party hosted by Donny Sutherland (remember him from Channel 7's 'Sounds Unlimited'?), the drummer and I found a bedroom, shut the door, locked it and stayed in that room making love for eight hours. Nonstop. We came out the next day and I remember Donny looking at me with a twinkle in his eye, as if to say, 'You're an animal.' But I didn't feel like an animal. I just felt really good. Somehow, though, after that look of Donny's, I felt quite embarrassed and shocked at what I had done in some stranger's home, not to mention a famous TV personality's home.

From then on, whenever I did 'Sounds Unlimited' on Saturday mornings, I'd get that look from Donny, as if to say, 'I remember, you wild girl.'

During one of my later trips to America in the mid-seventies I was introduced to a wealthy young black man. He used to pick me up from the studio and take me to dinner in these exotic luxury cars – Bentleys and Excaliburs and others (he had several). I remember being embarrassed by these cars, but I was fascinated by him. He was a frustrated guitar player and his future inevitably ended up in the business side of music. At that time, though, his wealth came from his father, who was one of the Mr Bigs of the 'black Mafia' in Los Angeles. (In fact, at one point in our relationship his father went to prison for a while.)

This young guy was an only child, and because of a lonely upbringing (his real mother, a jazz pianist, left him and his father when he was a baby) he had a real sadness about him. I was attracted to this. He wasn't like other black men I'd dated in America. Sure, he was conceited – why wouldn't he be? He was handsome, rich and smart – but he wasn't a show-off in the way others with much less to offer tended to be. For his part, he was constantly surprised by my lack of interest in his bank account. He'd never met a girl like me before. I also spoke my mind, which at the same time tickled *and* irritated him.

The first time we went out to dinner I ended up back in his apartment. It wasn't till the next day that I realised I'd got my period during the night. I was so mortified and embarrassed that I just wanted to get out of there; I didn't even help clean up or anything. I just said, *I have to go, I have to go.* That was it. Afterwards I regretted leaving so quickly, thinking that I'd never hear from him again. I really liked him.

But he, like my first-ever lover, persevered. He's the only other guy who has. He called the very next day and seemed to understand my embarrassment. After talking me into another dinner date, we began a year-long, tempestuous transatlantic relationship. Apart from the love-making, the best thing about our time together was our conversations about music. He had exquisite taste and introduced me to the records of some of the best singers and musicians in the world.

But we argued a lot ... What else is new? He was very domineering and I was much too opinionated for him. So when he hinted about the possibility of marriage, I realised I was not prepared to water down my personality, leave Australia and move into his mysterious life. It scared me. I eventually stopped calling and writing to him. It wasn't until almost nine years later, when I moved to New York, that I made contact with him again. He said to me, 'Do you know why it never worked out for us? Because you just wouldn't be My Woman.'

I've had some great times with some really wonderful men throughout my life, but I've always had a fear of rejection and consequently have ejected out of the aeroplane before it's crashed. Because of this I'm sure I've lost out on The One many times. There have been two men in my life who I've regretted not working harder to keep. One is no longer living, and the other is happily married with children and living overseas.

Romantically, I was always attracted to strong people. But I've always doubted the possibility of two strong characters being able to co-exist in complete harmony together without one or the other losing a bit of their identity. Somebody loses something, I believe. I guess, in this day and age, people talk about compromise and that's something I've just never been able to do. Or maybe I haven't been in love enough to want to compromise . . . I don't know.

In the end I'm a person who doesn't mind being 'alone'. I've been lonelier sometimes in a room full of people, or with a person at dinner, than by myself. To me, loneliness isn't who you're with, it's how you feel inside.

But I guess, deep down, I'm also a bit old fashioned in that I'm still looking for my soul mate. I'm comfortable being a single woman – in fact I think, apart from a few weak moments, I have it down to a fine art – but a little part of me is still searching for The One.

Chapter 12

MIRROR MIRROR ...

We all give off impressions. Sometimes they're exactly how we'd like them to be. Other times people derive impressions we've got no intention of giving off. I once ran into a guy who, years earlier, used to catch the same morning bus as me when I started going to work. He said he always used to stare at me because I looked so sophisticated, sexy and confident – all the things I actually didn't feel. I was sixteen.

A performer or a person in the public eye has all these complete strangers forming opinions about them, real or imagined. I know I've made things up about the people I've admired. When I was little and would make myself sing ten songs before going to sleep each night, I would imagine Paul McCartney was watching me. I'd look at a picture of him on the wall and imagine all sorts of things. Now it's hard to believe that I felt that way. But when you're in that idolatry condition and you gaze at somebody, a stranger that you admire, your imagination conjures up all sorts of things and you start believing them.

To this day, when I do interviews about the past, people say, 'Oh, you must have been raunchy.' I wasn't, really. There were some wild times, and I certainly joined in, but I'm more someone who *did*, not *was*, 'raunchy'.

My image is that of a wild, tough, heavy girl. People love a big, buxom woman standing up there, yelling. Men especially love to see a woman going off. Taken in by my performance, they would think that I was going off more than I really was. They probably imagined themselves at the other end of my going-off-ness. I was conscious, many times, of singing into that microphone and feeling the heat of men's eyes on my mouth, of them imagining that my microphone was their penis. They had never encountered a girl like me before; not in Australian pop music, anyway.

A lot of people used to think that's the way I always was, off stage as well as on: they imagined that I was really tough and ballsy. When I sang I gave off an air of being in control, but in reality I was just a girl – a girl with the same, if not more, doubts and insecurities as anyone. For me, the whole image thing was a constant burden.

Looking back, it's hilarious the things I did to achieve the image that I thought I *should* have had. Stupid things that a seemingly sane person wouldn't consider in a million years.

For instance, I've had a thing about my weight for the last twenty years or so, an obsession that has taken me on this amazing journey of weight losing (then gaining) and all the ridiculousness that comes with it.

Now, as a relatively pragmatic human being, I know that my friends and family love me as I am, regardless of what I weigh, but somewhere inside me I still feel as if I would be happier, and do better in my life generally, if I was slim. So it's been an ongoing battle.

First there were the diets.

There was the Israeli Diet, remember that one? It was nothing short of torture. You ate eggs and nothing but eggs one day, then meat and nothing but meat the next. There was also the Beverly Hills Diet, based on a similar idea, except this time you were only allowed to eat fruit – mainly pineapples. That one was hard to exist on in the real world: people had the runs so bad for the first few weeks, together with sores in their mouths from all the pineapples, no-one lasted long on that one. Of course you lost weight if you could stand it long enough ... *you were malnourished!* Then there was that food-combining diet where you ate only fruit up till midday and then carbohydrates or protein (but never both together) the rest of the time. There was also the Pritikin Diet. I can't remember much about that one, other than that its creator was murdered by his lover (a high school principal) somewhere in New York. I guess it was bad PR: subscribers dropped that diet like a bran hotcake!

It's amazing how most of these diets failed. They failed in the end because none of them provided good maintenance plans for everyday life, and they were all based on deprivation. But I kept on trying; I never lost faith in the hocus pocus of the diet trade. Weight Watchers has probably been the most returned-to diet for me, because it seems the most well-balanced plan. Unfortunately, though, a big, excitable and not very disciplined girl like me just can't seem to get enough of anything on any diet. I am passionate and irrational about food. It will always be my downfall.

It was while I lived in America between 1986 and 1994 that I gained most of my weight. Sitting waiting for the phone to ring will do it. It was a Catch 22 situation. At times I so wanted to get out and meet new people, but I felt so bad about my weight in the first place that I would stay home and gorge myself, almost to punish myself for being in this situation.

In America there's no end to the ideas they have to try to help you out when you're in this situation. They never give up on you, over there. No-one ever says, 'Forget it. Just stay fat.' If you've got a spare couple of hundred bucks, they're in your corner, trying to help.

In LA I had injections to reduce the fat content in my body. Looking back, I feel lucky to be alive. Who knows what they were injecting me with? I then went to a nutritionist who put me on a diet where all I could eat was protein. Nothing else. I went into a condition called ketosis as a result of a severe lack of potassium. My kidneys started to fail and I began to turn yellow, *but hell ... I was losing weight!* I had interviews in clinics where they hospitalise you and confine you to bed for two months like a sick person so you don't eat. I was desperate, but not that desperate ... I never went past the interview on that one. I went to fat farms. I even went to a psychiatrist. Prozac was prescribed, but it did nothing for my weight. (In fact, I felt so good on Prozac that I ate even more. It made me so happy.) I observed a meeting of Overeaters Anonymous, where people stood up and stated, 'Hi, my name is ... and I'm an overeater.' I wasn't having any of that.

I have to laugh sometimes when I hear, 'Maybe you don't want to lose the weight. Maybe you want to be fat.' Or, 'You're building a comfort zone around you because you've been hurt and it's a barrier between you and people.' Barrier schmarrier ... it's more like that pineapple doughnut I had for breakfast is the barrier! In the end I think my weight problems come down to two things: an inextinguishable passion for food, and the inability to concentrate and stay on one programme for long enough. Along with most other things in my life, if a diet is boring, I'll move on.

Despite the ups and downs of my weight and my self-esteem, somehow I still always woke up in a good mood, ready to take on the world. Every morning was a fresh hope to start again. I've been like that ever since I was a little girl: a bad day or night has never defeated me.

The worst of my psychological battles with my weight came from having to come back to Australia from the US for the odd tour. I'd have nightmares and be almost physically ill, knowing people hadn't seen me so large before and worrying what they'd say. You know when you see someone on TV who you haven't seen for a few years and they're completely blown up, and you say, 'Wow, they're fat! What happened? They used to look so good.' If I had rationalised it properly at the time I would have realised that, hey, that's the worst it can be: people commenting and then they move on. I guess the thing that horrified me most was that I'm the most opinionated person I know, and *I* was that person watching TV saying, 'Oh my God, what happened to her?'

I also hated the way people would pounce on a person who'd lost weight. I've been up and down in weight enough times to have learned that people can't wait to tell you that even though you're now fabulous, boy were you horrible before! And they dwell on this, thinking that the person that you've slimmed down to must be a different person inside too. But you are the same person that you were six months ago when you were fat, being incredibly insulted by this person using the licence of the fact that you've lost weight to say this stuff. In different ways, you had as much fun in your overweight body as you did with your slim body, but you're being treated as if in the fat old days nothing could have been good in your life. It's almost like they're mocking an old friend.

This transition in people's attitudes towards me extends to their ideas about my sexuality, too. I've been big *and* small over the years, lost weight and put it back on, and I've seen people's perceptions rise and fall with my weight. I'll go from a vamp in the bedroom, to Auntie Renée who would probably make the bed for the vamp. I can tell immediately how I'm perceived, and so I act accordingly. If they want an auntie, they'll get an auntie. (I give good auntie.) Unfortunately, I have the same taste in men as an auntie as I did as a vamp, and this is why I'm single. I haven't been willing to settle for what an auntie would get as a partner.

Every now and again you get the male who actually *loves* the large, round, voluptuous woman. He finds her a sexual turn-on. He's usually a tiny man who wants to be smothered in flesh. When you see him coming his eyes register like a Donald Duck cartoon, but instead of dollar signs in the eyeballs it's two large boobs: *DOOYNNGG!* If it's not the tiny fleshmonger who's after you, it's a big biker type. Some guys just live and breathe for a big bum, big tits and an attitude. They think they've died and gone to heaven. Unfortunately, these guys are rarely my type. I'd rather be on my own than be with someone who considers me a human fun park. Remember how I said I used to love Elvis? Yeah, well I get the Elvis type now ... the 'just before he died' Elvis type.

The press used to refer to me in terms like 'Aussie's very own leather-lunged belter' and 'Raunchy, robust Renée'. I didn't mind these labels, but I used to hate that there was no humour attached to them. There's nothing worse than a big, boisterous woman without any humour. I guess, in those days, it didn't show through, what with all my shyness and pretending to look tough.

On stage in those days I just closed my eyes and sang, shutting out the audience. I'm more relaxed now, so I guess my personality comes through. As I've progressed through my life I've reached a point where I now look forward to each gig because of the audience. For many years I dreaded gigs. I'd have fans, but they would be radio fans. I still get some of these people, but they're slowly being replaced by people who get the gist of all my music, not just the Top 40 stuff. Now, when I'm up on stage, I'm less self-conscious than I ever used to be, and I can feel people waiting for every song, not just the hits. They seem to trust me with my choice of songs. I can throw something in to surprise them and they welcome it.

A major career-changing review of one of my performances came in 1988 on one of my trips back from America. I did a little stint at Kinselas and the reviewer, who apparently hadn't seen me since some show in the seventies, wrote that I had gone away a blowsy blues shouter and come back a star. I think it changed a lot of people's perceptions about me, and it gave me a bit of an ego boost. (I did, however, find it amusing that my early career was described so unflatteringly. It's a very Australian thing: you never get a kiss on your lips without a slap on the head, just in case you get too big for your boots.)

My audiences are my real critics, however, and I've learned to appreciate them more and more as the years have gone by. In recent times I've noticed more independent women in my audiences. Some of them might have husbands and kids, but they are their own women. These are women who have the confidence to be part of something their husbands and children aren't, without feeling guilty about it. If I do a gig where everyone's sitting in their seats and there's a little space where people are able to dance, when I invite people to get up it's always the women who do. I often get knowing smiles and feel a strong kinship with them.

I think I have as many men fans as women fans, but these days men are more shy about showing their admiration. In my youth the men were a lot more up front about it, probably because then it was a sexual thing as well. Now it's more a musical respect I get from them, but it's nearly always the women who come out and let themselves be known.

Inasmuch as I'm proud of these girls, because they make me feel so good about what I do, some also make me embarrassed and a bit sad. I get some women at my shows, usually about my age, women who have been corralled into a life that they're not necessarily thrilled with. I'm their link back to a time when they were free and had choices. They think I've lived the kind of life they would have probably liked to live. (What they don't realise is that I feel sometimes like I've missed out on the stuff they have ...) Occasionally they get to drinking and become maudlin to the point where they're crying and inconsolable. One of them actually screamed at me at one of my shows recently, 'You owe me! I've been a fan and bought your records for twenty-five fucking years ... You owe me!'

Drunken fans like this usually want to come backstage after the show to explain themselves. Knowing that there's absolutely nothing I could say to them to make them feel better in the state they're in, I get poor old Shane, my sound guy, or some security guy, to tell them I've gone.

There were times when I *did* let people backstage, but I've learned from my mistakes. They come back and they want to talk about something you've touched in them, like you're a qualified counsellor or something. Or they want you to be the person that moaned 'You Broke a Beautiful Thing' on stage ten minutes ago. I can never be that person off stage. On stage, a magical thing happens to me, almost like a sort of channelling. Back in the dressing room, however, I can't be their mother confessor; I can't be that person they want me to be. I'm more like Dawn Lake: *How ya goin', luv?* People are shattered.

I got a letter from a disgruntled fan once. He wrote to me via my mother's address. He was saying how disgusted he was with how slovenly I looked. Couldn't I brush my hair better? Couldn't I wear better clothing? And then he added, 'like Melissa Manchester.' Until then, I might almost have agreed with him, but even my mother's reaction was, 'Melissa Manchester?!? What a Stupid!!'

I care that someone has an opinion about me, but not enough to rush off to a hairdresser to get a new hairdo. I've tried many times to doll up according to someone else's vision, and I've ended up looking like Mr Ed. Thankfully, though, I never get asked to change my music. It's been the one consistent throughout my life that seems to have pleased everybody, and it's given me the confidence to keep getting up and putting on 'the act'.

Those of us who tread the showbiz boards are a neurotic lot. Public perception is paramount in our world, and the public decide if you're going to make money or not. You're bound to get a little mixed up in the never-ending pursuit of what you think makes *them* happy. All the same, for the first time ever, I'm at a time in my life where I want to make myself happy. Sure, I'm still treading the boards, still on diets, still as neurotic as ever. But now I'm not so concerned by what people think of me. And I still wake up in a good mood every day.

DISCOGRAPHY

Sun '72
          Released in 1972 (RCA)
Renée Geyer
          1973 (RCA)
It's A Man's Man's World
          19 Aug 1974 (RCA Australia)
Ready To Deal
          24 November 1975 (RCA/Mushroom)
Really Really Love You (Live At The Dallas Brooks Hall)
          23 Aug 1976 (RCA/Mushroom)
Moving Along
          16 May 1977 (RCA/Mushroom)
Renée Geyer At Her Very Best
          12 December 1977 (RCA/Mushroom)
Winner
          11 December 1978 (RCA/Mushroom)
Blues License
          25 June 1979 (RCA/Mushroom)

So Lucky
        7 Dec 1981 (Mushroom)
Renée Live
        2 May 1983 (Mushroom)
Faves
        16 Jan 1984 (Mushroom)
Sing To Me
        1 July 1985 (WEA)
Renée Live at the Basement
        1986 (ABC Records)
Easy Pieces
        1988 (A&M Records)
Difficult Woman
        1994 (Larrikin)
The Best Of Renée Geyer – 1973-1998
        11 May 1998 (Mushroom)
Sweet Life
        1 March 1999 (Mushroom)